Thomas Erskine

The Spiritual Order

And other Papers. Third Edition

Thomas Erskine

The Spiritual Order
And other Papers. Third Edition

ISBN/EAN: 9783337332242

Printed in Europe, USA, Canada, Australia, Japan

Cover: Foto ©Lupo / pixelio.de

More available books at **www.hansebooks.com**

THE SPIRITUAL ORDER

AND OTHER PAPERS.

Edinburgh: Printed by Thomas and Archibald Constable,

FOR

DAVID DOUGLAS.

LONDON	. .	HAMILTON, ADAMS, AND CO.
CAMBRIDGE	. .	MACMILLAN AND BOWES.
GLASGOW . .	. . . .	JAMES MACLEHOSE AND SONS.

THE SPIRITUAL ORDER

AND OTHER PAPERS

SELECTED FROM THE MANUSCRIPTS

OF THE LATE

THOMAS ERSKINE OF LINLATHEN

THIRD EDITION

EDINBURGH
DAVID DOUGLAS
1884

PREFATORY NOTE.

THE circumstances in which this volume is given to the public call for some explanation.

Under the ever increasing infirmities of very advanced age, its author was unable to satisfy his own demand for unity and sequence in the utterance of his thoughts, and while he lived it would probably never have seen the light. Yet he felt he had a message for his generation, and he left it as his dying charge that his papers should be put into such order as was possible, that what was deemed suitable might be published.

Nothing more than arrangement and selection has been attempted. It has been regarded as a sacred duty to alter nothing and to add nothing. Where a few words seemed absolutely wanting they have been put within square brackets. The only liberty taken, beyond verbal corrections, has been the occasional suppression of a passage which seemed more in place or better expressed elsewhere. Several of these abstracted paragraphs have been added as Fragments.

To those who feel their need of some help amidst the perplexities of the age, the book is offered with the confident hope that it will be found to contain much very precious guidance both for the spirit and understanding.

EDINBURGH, *May* 1871.

CONTENTS.

	PAGE
I. THE SPIRITUAL ORDER, . .	1
II. THE DIVINE SON, . .	28
III. THE PURPOSE OF GOD,	47
IV. THE BIBLE IN RELATION TO FAITH, .	76
V. THOUGHTS ON ST. PAUL'S EPISTLE TO THE ROMANS,	100

FRAGMENTS :—

I. THE CLAIMS OF JESUS,	231
II. "BLESSED ARE THE POOR IN SPIRIT,"	233
III. WHAT IS RIGHTEOUSNESS?	234
IV. JUSTIFICATION,	237
V. FORGIVENESS,	238
VI. THE GOSPEL NO CHANGE IN THE PURPOSE OF GOD,	241
VII. GOD'S PURPOSE FOR US IS RIGHTEOUSNESS,	242
VIII. THE MEANING OF SALVATION,	243
IX. THE FATHER REVEALED IN THE SON,	243
X. THE TRUST OF CHRIST,	246
XI. CHRIST THE HEAD OR REPRESENTATIVE OF MAN, .	247

		PAGE
XII.	THE SACRIFICE WHICH PUTS AWAY SIN,	250
XIII.	LIFE THROUGH DEATH,	251
XIV.	THE DEATH OF CHRIST—JUDAS,	252
XV.	SIN,	255
XVI.	INNATE GOOD AND EVIL,	257
XVII.	THE TRUE IDEA OF "NATURAL RELIGION,"	258
XVIII.	"BY THIS SHALL ALL MEN KNOW THAT YE ARE MY DISCIPLES,"	260

I.

THE SPIRITUAL ORDER.

In the Introduction to his *Life of Jesus* M. Renan gives it as his opinion that Strauss has written his book on the same subject too much as a theologian and too little as an historian. He may be right in his criticism; yet I cannot conceive that the subject could be properly treated without a considerable introduction of theological thought, and accordingly it appears to me that the want of such thought is a radical defect in M. Renan's own work.

The avowed purpose of the appearing of Jesus on earth, and of all that he said and did, was to proclaim "the kingdom of heaven"—the supremacy and reign of God and of His holy will—to call men to come into it and to submit themselves to it, as their only escape from sin and misery and confusion. That they might understand its nature, and how much it was to be longed for, he revealed the Father ; that is, he taught that God, the King of that kingdom, was the loving, righteous Father of every man. This being the purpose of his appearance on the earth, his life can surely never be rightly understood apart from this purpose, and from the very remarkable way in which he carried it out. His life cannot be separated from his teaching ; and when we say that his life has affected the world's history more than any other life that was ever lived in it, we mean that in what he *was*, interpreted by what he taught, a power lay which produced these results.

That teaching had in it much that commended itself to the reason and conscience of its Jewish hearers, containing as it did the highest and purest morality ; but this, though superior in degree, was not dissimilar in kind to what they had been accustomed to hear from the old teachers of their nation. The peculiarity of his teaching—the startling novelty of it—the dissimilarity in it to anything which they had ever heard before, consisted mainly in certain claims which he made for himself;

in a claim to be not *a* son of God but *the* Son of God, and in a claim to be the Head and Lord and Saviour of men. I say, claims which he made for *himself*; and yet his own constant explanation of them was that in making them he was not seeking his own glory but revealing the Father, not only His fatherly character and purpose towards men but His relation to them, and this with a living fulness unattainable in any other way.

This is what M. Renan in the first place condemns as "self-preaching," and then summarily puts aside as incredible because supernatural. He evidently considers that the moral teaching of Jesus constitutes the substance and essence of Christianity, and that it would have been really a better and purer thing had it been unmixed with those "*visionary personal pretensions.*" Though the fourth Gospel is almost exclusively occupied with this self-preaching, and though there are few chapters in the other three in which it does not appear, he yet passes over this distinguishing feature of the teaching without any earnest attempt to explain it; for we cannot give such a name to the mere suggestion that Jesus had in his own mind so completely identified himself with his moral teaching that he felt as if he were only inculcating *it* when he spoke of himself, that he was but repeating the precepts of the Sermon on the Mount when he said " I am the true Vine," or " I am the Bread that came down from heaven." This is evidently impossible and unreasonable; it would be more true to say that he considered all his teaching as summed up in the exposition of his own personal relation to God and man—and thus that he identified his teaching with his personality—than that he identified his personality with his teaching. He is the Vine, and it is only by abiding in him that we can bring forth spiritual fruit. He is the Bread that came down from heaven, and it is by feeding on him that the soul is nourished unto eternal life. He is the Shepherd of the sheep; he is the Door through which alone they can enter into the fold.

" The Father judgeth no man, but hath committed all judgment to the Son, that all men should honour the Son even as they honour the Father." " Before Abraham was, I am." These are high claims; yet, though pressed and insisted on continually, they were always, as I have said, accompanied with a protest that in making them he was not seeking his own glory but was revealing the Father—that he was dependent on the Father for all things— that he knew nothing and could do nothing of himself—that it was the Father dwelling in him who did the works—that he had not come of himself, but that the Father had sent him—and that no man could come to him except by the drawing of the Father: thus showing that his self-preaching was no self-exaltation but a real revelation of the Father, because holding him forth as the Author and Mover of all that he, the Son, did. Moreover, these claims are made in such a truthful, unexaggerated, unboastful tone, in a tone of such entire conviction and of such perfect mental soundness, that no reasonable man can feel himself entitled to throw them away without the deepest consideration, and in fact rarely does throw them away without a lurking suspicion that there is something in them which has as yet escaped his intelligence.

However incredible these claims might appear to M. Renan, yet surely when he undertook to write the *Life of Jesus* he was bound to examine whether Jesus really made them; and, if he did, to consider what purpose he could have had in making them. But he does nothing of the kind; he neither expresses any doubts as to their having been made by Jesus, nor does he attempt to give any explanation of them beyond that most unsatisfactory one to which I have referred above. He does not accuse Jesus of being either a fanatic or a deceiver; on the contrary he expresses the highest admiration for him both morally and intellectually; he thinks him "the best and wisest and greatest man that ever lived." Now is it not strange that he does not make some serious attempt to understand what this best and wisest and greatest man could have meant when he made such claims for himself? It has been said that even the mistakes of great men would repay examination by suggesting some truth which they were aiming at but had missed. And surely one would have expected from the historian of Jesus, especially from one who expresses such admiration of him, that he would to the utmost of his ability have investigated and analysed a mistake, if mistake it be, which has had such an influence on the world, and which has taken such a hold on the minds of men ever since its first promulgation.

But M. Renan does not believe that there is anything reasonable in theology, and therefore does not give himself what he would deem the fruitless labour of seeking for it. He doubtless received his earlier conceptions of Christianity from his Church in blind and unquestioning submission, and was taught to occupy himself with the detail of its observances, and the external authority on which it was founded, and by which it must be defended, rather than with its actual spirit and meaning. And when he subsequently rejected it, he probably did so not because he had studied it and had detected some unreasonableness or inconsistency in the principles developed in it, but simply because it pretended to be supernatural, and he had laid it down as an axiom that no such pretension could be admitted. In fact he knew nothing of Christianity but its beautiful morality and its miraculous pretensions. The first he could and did admire, not perhaps in its full sense but at least in an æsthetic fashion. The last appeared to him simply a manifestation of the ignorance and prejudice of the period, to which Jesus felt himself obliged to yield.

If he had so studied the Christian morality as to perceive that it consisted in qualities which could not be called forth by any amount of mere effort—in filial love and trust towards God producing all other goodness—he would have expected to find in Christian theology (supposing it to be logically consistent) such discoveries of the character of God and of His relation to man as would, when believed, naturally and without effort call forth such trust and love; and this expectation might have induced him to examine these claims of Jesus in the hope of finding such discoveries laid up in them. Had he so examined them he would have found that they not only make these discoveries, but also open up a view of the constitution and organisation of that spiritual order, the existence of which Christianity affirms; a view which, however wonderful, is perfectly coherent with the moral system, and with all that our reason and conscience recognise in God.

I will venture to say that until this consideration has been given, Christianity has not really been understood. I believe that the manifestation of self-sacrificing love on the part of God is its distinguishing feature, and is necessary as the only sufficient ground of that absolute trust which lies at the root of the Christian character; and I believe that it is only in the history of Jesus, taken in connection with these supernatural claims, that this self-sacrificing love is fully declared.[1] If we once catch a glimpse of a real meaning in these claims—if we once arrive at the conviction that there must be *relations* contained within the Being of God which may have their interpretation in them, and if we see how all this subserves the revelation of *the Father*—our confidence in the veracity of that noble and reverend character will help us onward to a firmer grasp, a fuller apprehension of the mystery.

It would have been a light to M. Renan had the thought suggested itself that a man would be helped in his endeavours to be patient under sorrow or suffering of any

[1] Appendix A.

kind, if he not only saw that such patience was a *duty*, but if he moreover accepted the *doctrine* that it was a loving Father who had appointed his lot, and who had a loving and wise purpose to accomplish by it. If, starting with this discovery, M. Renan had looked for a similar meaning in all doctrines, he might have been guided to the conclusion, that as a man cannot have the feelings of a good citizen nor fulfil the duties of one until he is in some measure acquainted with the traditions and constitution of his country and his own place in it; as he cannot enter into the feelings befitting the member of a family nor fulfil the duties of one until he learns the composition of the family, its traditions, and his own place in it; so if he belongs to a spiritual order he cannot acquire the feelings and character suitable to it, nor can he rightly fulfil its duties, until he is instructed in its constitution and history and his own position therein.

But are we really justified in assuming that there is a spiritual order to which as human beings we belong, and that we are capable of apprehending it? I believe that few of those who are likely to look into this book will feel any doubt as to this; yet I think it well to give the ground on which my own belief of it rests, without pretending either to demonstrate my view, or to refute that of others.

It seems to me then that the conscious demand within us for an inward goodness—for right feelings and intentions as well as right actions—always implies and supposes the existence of a spiritual order, or cosmos, to which we ourselves belong, and of which that inward goodness is the law. So far as mere social order is concerned, my morality is sufficient if I abstain from actions which injure society, and am diligent in the performance of actions which benefit it. But the consciousness of an obligation to possess and exercise moral qualities within my own secret heart, such as humility, purity, sincerity, and disinterested love to all men, refers me to an entirely different kind of order. These qualities do not seem necessary to a mere outward order; it could go on without them. They are spiritual qualities, and must belong to a spiritual order; and the consciousness that they are obligatory, and essential to my well-being, even more than the acts connecting me with the social order, proves both that a spiritual order does exist, and that I belong to it still more essentially than I do to the other. I belong to both, but the spiritual is the deeper; it underlies the other, and is independent of it; yet the two are not unconnected, for I find that I cannot perform any ordinary social act in a way which satisfies my conscience unless it is also done according to that spiritual order.[1]

Christianity assumes that this spiritual order exists, and that all men belong to it; and whilst in its precepts it declares the duties of its members, it gives in its theological doctrines such a discovery of the nature and constitution of this order as may consciously and powerfully influence those who apprehend

[1] The natural world is full of orders or systems composed of parts which when separated from their order lose all their meaning and power. Thus a tree is composed of branches and twigs, which, while they continue in their proper relation to it, bear leaves and flowers and fruits, but lose this power when separated from it. Their vitality does not reside in themselves, but must be received moment by moment from the root, and thus their vital completeness depends on the continuation of their healthy connection with the tree. Our spiritual completeness or incompleteness depends on the same principle, namely, the maintenance of relation to our order.

its reality, and thus qualify them for the performance of all duty.

If we belong to an order we must, as I have said, know something of its nature before we can be in a position to fulfil its duties; we cannot fulfil its duties without entering into its spirit, and we cannot enter into its spirit without knowing something of its nature and of our relation to it. This is, to a certain extent, true of all orders, but some are more organically constituted than others; that is, more connected with the very roots of our being, more like the relation of the branch to the vine, which, being absolutely essential to its life, necessarily embraces all its living actions. Thus, though a man cannot really fulfil the higher duties required of a citizen unless he is well acquainted with the constitution and traditions of the state, he may still, in a retired and private station, pass muster, so to speak, although his knowledge be very slight. But it is otherwise with the family order; for evidently, if he does not know his father and mother or his brothers and sisters, he cannot pass muster; he will be constantly committing blunders and proving himself at every turn unfit for the duties of his place. The reason of this difference is that the family relation is a more intimate one than the political, and makes more demands on the heart and inner life. But our relation to the spiritual world is the most inward and intimate of all our relations, and must therefore be the most organic. Much of the life of a family-man will be spent in pursuits of his own, unconnected with the family and requiring none of the family vitality in order to their being rightly carried out. Still more is this true in respect to citizenship. Whereas, as members of the spiritual order, we can do absolutely nothing right in thought, word, or deed, unless we do it in the life of our order and under the influence of our conscious relationship to it. For our relation to the spiritual order means in truth our relation to God, in whom and by whom we live, and without whom we can exercise no function of life either mental or physical; so that, not by any conventional or arbitrary appointment, but in very deed and in actual reality, we are dependent on Him at every moment, and our relation to Him has no interruption and no limits. Our conscious moral nature proves this relationship to us, "those thoughts which wander through eternity" prove it; and although we belong also to an outward superficial order, and have a life suited to it into which we can for a time so entirely throw ourselves as to shut out the thought of the higher order, yet we cannot put it from us; we belong to it essentially, and our chief good and ill must at all times be connected with it.

The theological part of a religion then only really commends itself to our reason when it has a true efficient correspondence with the preceptive part; that is, when it gives such a representation of the relation in which God stands to us as may have a direct tendency to produce in us that character which the preceptive teaching inculcates. When therefore we meet with a distinctive peculiarity in the preceptive part of a religion, we ought to expect something in its theological teaching which may correspond to it as its living root.

The coherent relation of the doctrines of Christianity to its moral precepts, and the dynamic efficiency of the doctrines in producing spontaneous obedience, and thus working out the Christian character, is one of the most striking evidences of the truth of Christianity.

In fact its philosophy—its reasonableness—consists in this relation; just as the evidence of the Newtonian theory consists in the relation of the law of gravitation to the orbits and movements of the planetary bodies. It is therefore only in the light of this relation that the doctrines have any true meaning, or are supported by any proper evidence.[1]

When we first awaken to the evil of sin, it seems to us that our business is to resist it in its manifestations, such as self-occupation, indifference to the feelings and interests of others, covetousness, etc., but we soon find

[1] The idea that anything is imposed on us by Christianity to be believed just for believing's sake, so to speak, and without any reference to the disclosure it makes of the mind of God towards us, or to its moral bearing on our character, must have a tendency to produce either infidelity or superstition. Accordingly, I cannot but think that the time-honoured use of creeds, in which all the articles of belief are crowded together without the smallest indication of their purpose, must have a very questionable tendency for many minds; especially when the idea is suggested, as in the Athanasian Creed, that there is a merit in believing that which to our reason appears incredible, and that our believing certain dogmas is the arbitrary condition on which God will bestow on us eternal life.

that the effect of all direct efforts to resist such tendencies is limited to the suppression of their outward actings, whilst the tendencies themselves remain as strong as before. The preceptive teaching of the Sermon on the Mount cannot be obeyed by mere effort, however sincere and however earnest, because it requires something more than the repression of evil actions and the performance of good actions; it does not merely forbid the outbreak of pride and vanity and selfishness; it requires inward humility, inward purity, inward love of God and of men, even of our enemies. Now, I am quite conscious that by efforts of self-restraint I can, at least to some extent, prevent the expression and outcoming of evil, but I am equally conscious that I cannot command the presence of the opposite spiritual qualities. I cannot, for example, by any effort love those who are hateful and despicable, although I may control every expression of dislike. I cannot make myself humble in heart and pure in heart. I cannot cast out the spirit of covetousness, or ambition, or vanity. I may see that it would be right and most desirable to do so; but I can no more

B

do it than I can command midnight to become midday.

A principle of love—a living love, the opposite of selfishness—is the only power which can enable me to be inwardly what I feel I ought to be, and to give free and spontaneous submission to all the demands of my conscience; yet love is a power which I cannot create or command within myself, which must come to me, if at all, from some outward source. I am thus brought to the conclusion that I am not complete in myself—that I have not within myself the means of being what I feel I ought to be—that I require a help, beyond what I find either in my reason or conscience, to enable me to be what both reason and conscience call on me to be. Surely then there must exist some means of escape from this incompleteness. Moreover it seems to me that the self-condemnation inseparable from the consciousness of incompleteness, even while we feel that we have striven against it with our best endeavours, is really a declaration from the Author of our being that such a means does exist, and that we are wrong when we are not possessing and using it.

It has often appeared to me remarkable that we should have this self-condemnation for faults and defects which belong to us, not by our own choice but sometimes by the very accident of birth, as much as the colour of our hair or any other physical peculiarity ; yet the laws of our spiritual being do compel us to condemn ourselves for them notwithstanding.

Is there righteousness in such compulsion ? Is it reasonable that I should be self-condemned for not being what with all my might I have endeavoured to be ? The only way in which I can justify to my own mind this instinctive self-condemnation is by realising that I am a creature of God, dependent on Him for my existence both natural and spiritual, and that He has so constituted me that the conscious recognition of this dependence is absolutely necessary to the rightness of all my moral and spiritual doings, not by any arbitrary appointment nor as a mere homage due to Him, but because this dependence is a great reality through the recognition of which I am brought into the conscious and continual apprehension of that love of God from which all my love must be derived.

Evidently this dependence, which belongs to me necessarily as a creature, is no defect,[1] but is the real relation through which alone all spiritual good can come to me ; and when I apprehend that through my consciousness of it my Creator and loving Father calls me into an uninterrupted fellowship with Himself, I can realise that He does not intend that I should feel it as a weakness or a bondage, but on the contrary as a strength, and an honour, and a joy ; indicating, as it does, the nearness and dearness of my relation to Him.[2] I can now acknowledge the justice of this instinctive self-condemnation, because I see that I am myself shutting out the love which can alone fulfil the law so long as I act as if I were self-existing or self-sufficient, so long as I en-

---

[1] I have sometimes thought that those who composed the prayer of confession in the beginning of the Genevese Liturgy had forgotten this great principle. In that formula the worshippers are taught to say : "Nous confessons, que nous sommes de pauvres pécheurs, nés dans la corruption, inclins au mal, *incapables, par nous-mêmes, de faire du bien.*" The expression seems to indicate that they would have thought themselves in a better condition if they had been "capables par eux-mêmes de faire du bien." The authors of the prayer probably meant merely to express their sense of man's dependence on God for the power of doing well, and had no conception that the words in their natural sense seemed to express a regret that this was his condition.

[2] Appendix B.

deavour to do by the mere force of independent volition, what I *can* only do by an influence received from God moment by moment, the influence, let me call it, of spiritual gravitation.

Suppose a planet gifted with intelligence and volition, on the strength of this gift emancipating itself from the law of gravitation —it would soon find that all its sweet order and harmony were gone, and that its independent efforts to perform its revolution could not do the work of a centre of gravity. Its completeness consists in the maintenance of its relation to this centre, without which all goes wrong.

Man's conscience, used rightly, is the organ of his relation to the great spiritual Centre, and the channel through which the guiding and sustaining influences of that centre are communicated to him; but when he attempts to use it independently—to obey the light of conscience without recognising the sun out of which its light comes, and thus to sever himself from his true centre—he is made to feel that independent effort cannot do the work which conscience requires. That work is loving spontaneous work, and there is no love of the kind to be had in the universe except in that centre. *There* therefore he must seek and find it, for love alone can give him rightness and order and blessedness.

It is not a chart of its course which a planet needs to keep it in its orbit, but a centre of gravity and a law of gravitation. The planet has its proper centre imposed on it, and is kept by an irresistible necessity in its orbit, without any need for its own concurrence or co-operation. Man also has his proper centre, but as he is a voluntary being he must choose it for himself, it cannot be imposed upon him. As God is the true eternal centre of his spiritual life, for whom and in whom he was created, so, by the law of his being, while he remains in his true relation to Him everything that he does will necessarily be right, and when he separates himself from Him everything will necessarily be incomplete and defective. He does need a chart of his course: in the first place perhaps to teach him that he cannot follow its guidance by independent effort, and secondly that, by comparing the course he is pursuing with his chart, he may be in a condition to judge whether he has chosen the right centre and is obeying the true law. But it is in our relation to God, rightly observed, that our whole strength lies, so that in casting off His rule we really cast off the power of being right; and thus, though endowed with will, we are, in this respect, under a law of necessity.

"Our wills are ours to make them Thine."

We cannot be right by a *direct effort of will*, but only by adhering, in the exercise of that will, to our true centre; that is, by dependence on God. So that the proper action of the human will is to choose the right centre.

But how are we to learn to make this right choice? By becoming acquainted with our spiritual order, that is (translating the expression into life), by learning to know God, that so we may trust Him fully and love Him fully. And we must know Him, not only as One whose righteousness we can understand and entirely approve, but also as One who loves us and whom we can love; for love is the only completeness, and love can be called forth only by a Being whom we can approach and know and love. We cannot love a law or an abstraction, nor can we love a Being whose mind and purposes towards ourselves we cannot apprehend and trust.[1] It is only by the discovery of this knowability and accessibility in God's nature that we can really learn to love Him, and it is only through love that the mere sense of duty—the desire to be right—can be developed into the spontaneous love of right; and until this development takes place, we remain in our incompleteness.

In order to feel assured that we are right in requiring this character in God, we have only to consider what His love has to do in us. In the first place, we must find in it a real joy—a satisfying portion—which, by filling the desires of our hearts, will elevate us above the cravings of ambition and sensuality and covetousness and vanity. For the seductive power of these propensities lies in the assurance which they offer to our imaginations of a present gratification to be derived from yielding to

---

[1] I believe that those who insist most strongly on the importance of ascribing personality to God really mean this. The term itself seems to the logical intellect to imply limitation, which is perhaps the reason why some are so much opposed to the use of it. I would not dispute about a word, but I am persuaded that the whole spirit and power of Christianity are contained in *the thing which is meant by the word.*

them; and it is only by knowing and possessing a purer and more abiding joy in God that we can successfully resist them. We may with our whole souls condemn and fight against them, nay even despise them, but until that place in our hearts which they seek to occupy is already better filled, we are never safe from their assaults. Moreover, we must find a *power* in His love which will enable us actually to love those who are unloveable—whom our very consciences condemn—but who yet as human beings have a claim upon our love; that is, we must find in His love a fountain out of which our own hearts may be ever replenished with the same love.

Now how is this to be accomplished? Why thus: We know how unworthy we ourselves are of God's love, yet He loves us; for His is a love which is not repelled by unworthiness, but seeks to deliver from unworthiness, and to make all men worthy. That is its nature. It is a righteous love which ever seeks to communicate itself. Well, He loves me in my unworthiness, and He loves my hostile brother as He loves me, both of us in our unworthiness; and His purpose is to make us worthy of His love and of each other's love; and His will for both is that we should know this as His purpose and co-operate with Him in carrying it out. He invites me to ascend by that ray of love which comes to me from His heart, and from that central heart, in the light of its love, to see and to appreciate and to love my brother.

Evidently, such love as this can only be called forth by a personal Being; that is to say, we cannot so love a law or an abstraction.[1] For surely the satisfying object of man's conscience can never be a mere rule or standard of right which only shows him his duty, but must be a living power which will enable him to reach that standard.

Thus man never finds his right place in the

[1] It may at first sight appear that a love possessing this personal character, though it may be more powerful and efficient than the simple and unmixed choice of abstract right, is for that very reason necessarily less pure, but I believe that there can be no such thing as an abstract righteousness, that it is really *impossible* to separate the idea of righteousness from the idea of a living will; and that, therefore, God—*the living righteousness*, and not any such abstraction—is the true object of man's conscience. God is not merely a Being who is righteous, but *the very being—the living and personal fountain—of righteousness.* The Greek teachers speak of τὸ δίκαιον, "righteousness," but the Hebrew Scriptures always speak of "the righteous One." This last, I believe, is the truest philosophy as well as the only religion.

spiritual world until he not only sees and approves the way of righteousness, but until the object of his conscience becomes also the object of his trust and love ; in a word, until *he finds God, and discovers that the kingdom of heaven is the kingdom of his Father.*

II.

THE DIVINE SON.

Man being the chief work of God with which we are acquainted, his education—his moral and rational development—is the highest purpose of God that we can conceive. But the existence of such a purpose implies the existence of that in the nature of God which is necessary to its accomplishment, for we cannot suppose that if it exists it will remain unaccomplished. Yet it must remain for ever unaccomplished, unless God is a Being who may be known, One who attracts and draws forth the trust and sympathy and love of the creature made in His image.

And if this knowledge of the Divine nature is necessary to the education of man, we are prepared to find that it has been communicated to him in such a way as to distinguish it from the products of his own mind, and mark it as coming direct from God. If a man felt that he had wrought out the true idea of God and of the spiritual order by his own faculties, it would be to him a philosophy in which he took an intellectual interest rather than a religion which dominated his spirit. Abstract thoughts can never sink into the heart of humanity, and can give rise only to the dogmas of a school, not to a religion for the race.

Evidently such a revelation, being thus essential to God's chief purpose, is not merely not incredible, but on the contrary is in the highest reason to be looked for ; and whatever its form may be, it must in its substance be *supernatural*, being a revelation of God ; and yet it ought not to be considered *preternatural*, being only the coming forth of a higher nature.

Any one who really apprehends the superiority of the spiritual over the material is prepared to believe that the natural laws which reign in the world of matter, such as gravitation, electricity, and chemical affinities, belong to a lower order; and that underlying and overruling these are the true eternal laws, which can be nothing else than God's own mind and character,—His wisdom, love, and righteousness. There is therefore no reason to be astonished if, in that greatest work of educating spiritual intelligences, those outward laws give place to the deeper, especially when the object to be attained is the communication of the knowledge of Himself.

Christianity, though a divine revelation, did not profess to reveal—and did not in point of fact reveal—anything which has not a response in man's spiritual intelligence, and of the truth of which his reason and conscience cannot judge; so that we are never left entirely dependent on external authority for any of its statements. These statements refer to relations in which we actually stand to God and to the spiritual world. It does not *make* the relations, it only calls our attention to them; we are created in them, they enter into the very substance of our spiritual organisation, so that there must be a consciousness of them within us, dormant and torpid, perhaps, but capable of being awakened and quickened by the proper application. In fact, these communications could never enter into us nor influence us, unless there were in our original constitution a capacity for apprehending them, through the possession of faculties and instincts corresponding to the relations to which they refer.

This principle will be readily admitted in reference to the doctrine of the existence of God, and of His relation to men as a loving, righteous Father, by many who would yet hesitate to admit that they have actual grounds in reason and conscience, apart from all authority, for believing in the claims of Jesus to be the Son of God, and to be the Head and Lord and Saviour of men.[1]

I believe that the fatherly relation and pur-

---

[1] Those of my readers who know the essay on the Incarnation in the series of *Tracts for Priests and People* are already acquainted with the train of thought here developed. As I read that essay, it commended itself to my mind as one of the most important contributions to theological science which had been made in our day. And if I may judge of its author's feelings by my own, I believe that he will be gratified by finding that any other person had independently been led to the same conclusions. I had from an early period learned to see how the character and mission of Christ met the needs of men, but I always felt the just demands of my reason unsatisfied until I saw how that character and mission were really implied in the Divine Nature itself.

pose of God towards men is the fundamental revelation of Christianity, and that all other true doctrines can only be explanatory and illustrative, or corroborative of it. The loving purpose of God to educate men into a moral sympathy with Himself and with one another, is the light which I require to see in a religious doctrine in order that I should believe it. I must see a reasonableness in it, that is, I must see that it harmonises both with the nature and character of God, and with man's spiritual needs and instincts. Now, do I see such a reasonableness in the doctrine of the divinity of Jesus Christ? I think I do, to this extent, that I am sure there must be a distinction in the Divine nature analogous to that of Father and Son, whether Jesus be that Son or not, and I shall endeavour to explain my conception, praying the reader to give me his calm and unprejudiced attention.

What, then, is Jesus Christ? We have been taught to answer, He is the eternal Son of the Father. But what do these words mean? What is the meaning of the *eternal Son of the Father?* We ought surely to ask this question, for we must be sure that if Christianity is a revelation of God, every part of it, especially so marked a feature in it as this, must have a meaning most important for us to understand, because it is connected with the character of God and our relation to Him.

Jesus himself proposed the question, What think ye of the Christ; whose son is he? The hearers did not seem to understand its importance, and he did not press it; but by putting the question he has left it as a legacy to all generations, and we are not justified in passing it by or remaining satisfied with a merely formal answer. Christ preached himself even more than he preached duties, as if the knowledge of him were really the efficient power by which alone duties could be performed.

But is there anything, apart from this self-preaching, which could guide us to the idea of there being a Father and a Son in the Divine nature? I would answer: Amongst the thoughts concerning God which necessarily present themselves to our minds, a very prominent one is that He is the living Fountain of goodness—that all goodness is in Him, and that there is no goodness which is not in Him,

c

If we take the word, "None is good, save One, that is God," as the declaration of an absolute truth, then wherever we see goodness we ought to consider it as belonging to Him and flowing from Him, and as a manifestation of His presence.

But in following out this principle, we are conducted to consequences which we may at first feel some hesitation in admitting. There is a goodness in trust, as there is a goodness in trustworthiness; there is a goodness in receiving, as there is a goodness in giving; there is a goodness in obeying rightly, as there is a goodness in ruling rightly. Most assuredly these are both forms of goodness, but shall we say that they both exist in God? Shall we say that obedience and submission and gratitude and trustful dependence can be predicated of Him, or shall we say that though these qualities are good in the creature they are inconsistent with the sovereignty of the Creator? If we come to the latter decision, we at once admit that there may be goodness which has not its source in God. I am persuaded that the highest and truest reason will adhere to the principle that there can be no goodness of which God is not the proper fountain. And if so, we must also admit that for every active form of goodness in God there is a corresponding recipient form ; consequently that there must be in the Divine nature distinct personalities representing these two forms, otherwise there could be no possibility either of their exercise or of their manifestation in Himself apart from the creature.

It is true that both these classes of qualities may and often do exist in one and the same person : thus the most generous giver will often be the most grateful receiver ; but they cannot be in correlative activity in one person : a man cannot be grateful or obedient or trustful to himself ; above all, he cannot have sympathy with himself. Now if it be granted that the very nature of God is Love, and that love necessarily seeks sympathy, shall we not feel that it is even absurd to suppose that, *in consequence of His unity*, God should not have that sympathy *within* His own nature, and that He should be, as it were, compelled to create in order to have it ? And is there not a real relief in the doctrine of the Eternal Sonship as a deliverance from the thought of a God whose very nature is love dwelling in absolute solitude from all eternity without an object of love? I am aware that the answer to this suggestion will be that we make a God after our own image, and then reason on our own creation. But if we were intended to know God and to live in relations with Him (and that we are, the history of the race, as well as each man's consciousness, abundantly testifies), it is impossible to arrive otherwise at any idea whatever of God. The only goodness and the only intelligence that we can conceive of are human goodness and intelligence, and we are obliged just to expand these into infinity when we would form to ourselves an idea of God.[1] And seeing that we are constrained by reason to acknowledge that all goodness must be in God, we ought not to refuse the suggestion that there must be, as it were, two hemispheres in the Divine nature,—upper and under, active and passive, Giver and Receiver, Father and Son. Unity is not singleness but rather completeness, and love can only, by minds like

---

[1] But when we have done this, is it possible for us to believe that this idea is merely the creation of our own minds, and not an eternal reality that has revealed itself to us? It is assuredly an eternal reality.

ours, be considered complete when it has sympathy.

This idea of God as comprehending both the active and the passive of all goodness, distinguished by the personalities of Father and Son but united in one common Spirit, seems to me to give the perfect conception of love and of blessedness in love ; and when we add the idea that the spiritual creation stands in the Son, we have the assurance that it also is intended to be included in that fellowship of love.

This conception of the eternal relation of the Son to the Father has a remarkable agreement with the language of our Lord, which indeed is otherwise scarcely intelligible ; for he not only says, "I and my Father are one," but also, "My Father is greater than I," which last cannot mean merely that though as God he was equal with the Father yet as man he was inferior, for of this inferiority there could be no possible doubt ; it required no messenger from above to tell us this. But we did need a Divine teacher to help us to look into the very nature of God, and there to see an eternal Giver and an eternal Receiver of all the fulness of God. When St. John wrote "God is Love," he was no doubt contemplating the Divine Father pouring out the eternal treasures of His love and wisdom into the all-embracing and all-sympathising capacity of the Divine Son, who receives it not for himself alone, but as the Head and First-Begotten of the whole creation.

The idea of the Fatherhood of God was present in most of the ethnic religions, and is implied in all the Old Testament Scriptures; yet it is clear that even the Jewish people regarded God rather as a Sovereign—a Lawgiver and Judge—than as a Father. It remained for the gospel of Jesus Christ to make this revelation.[1] There can be no full and perfect revelation of Fatherhood but in and through Sonship, and thus the revelation of an eternal Son in the Divine nature itself,—a Son in whom the whole spiritual family has its root and standing,—gives an assurance of the unchangeable fatherly relation of God to man which nothing

---

[1] In fact, the universal Fatherhood of God is the real scope of the gospel; but this Fatherhood will be a mere honorary title till we realise that we are created in the Son, that so we may be actual partakers with him in the filial relation to his and our Father.

else could have given. And the appearance on earth of this eternal Son—one with the Father and the express image of His person—in our nature, bearing all our burdens with a love which tasted death for every man, and with a filial confidence in the love of Him who imposed the burdens which never failed, this was the highest conceivable manifestation of the trustworthiness of the Father. When we think of this Being as possessing all wisdom and all power, we can rejoice to know that He is our God, the Maker, the Sustainer, the Appointer of all things. We can feel assured that He must create only for good, and that especially when He creates moral intelligences, it must be with the purpose of bringing them into a participation of that same eternal sympathy.

Now let us think what the right place must be for such moral intelligences to occupy. If they are created to be good, and if there is no goodness but of God, surely their goodness must be that of the Son,—loving and sympathising obedience, trustful dependence, a filial will entering into and adopting the purpose of the Father; and their capacity of goodness must consist in the indwelling of the Son, whose presence in them both confers on them his own filial relation to the Father and communicates to them the character of his own goodness. Thus we see how Christian morality rises out of and is dependent on Christian theology; and how those precepts which direct the doing of the most ordinary actions of humanity have, according to the Christian theory, their root in these claims of Jesus.[1]

There seems to have been a preparation in the Jewish mind for the idea of a Son of God; that is, they seem to have believed that there is such a being, although their conceptions on the subject were extremely vague. What are ours?

It has been my purpose all along to show that any doctrine which is received simply on authority and not because we see its truth, is not rightly received; and I have maintained this, not with the desire of elevating man's confidence in his own understanding, but because it seems evident that until the truth of a doctrine is apprehended by, and actually comes in contact with, the spiritual under-

[1] Appendix B.

standing, it cannot with propriety be said to be believed, and cannot rightly influence the character. Does this principle hold good in reference to our belief of the Divine nature or proper Deity of Christ, or must *this* doctrine at all events be received simply on the authority of an external revelation? I have often wondered at the large and general acceptance which it has met with; and I have asked myself whether this acceptance was due to a blind and unreflecting following of authority or whether there is some deep principle in our nature which responds to it and welcomes it as that which satisfies its craving. I am persuaded that the last explanation is true; for assuredly there is a demand within us to see on the throne of the universe a Being who can sympathise with us, and with whom we can sympathise; assuredly the consciousness of sin makes us welcome a Mediator—a "Days man"—seated there, partaking both of the nature of Him from whom we have been alienating ourselves, and of our own, and in whom—the true Son of Man—we may draw near to the Father. I am also persuaded that those who have profitably received this doctrine have always seen some light in it, even when they could not have said very distinctly what that light was, and that none have ever really believed in the Divine nature of Jesus and in his relation to men, who have not first seen there that which has helped them to know and trust and love the Father.

Moreover, they have felt that men are not intended to be mere separate units but to form an organised body, and that they must have a Head uniting them both to God and to each other, and therefore partaking of both natures. This seems indeed to be an instinctive conviction of the human mind, manifesting itself in the hero-worship which has kept its ground amidst all the risings and fallings of religious opinion. Men feel that they need one in whom they can glory, and to whose guidance they can trust themselves—one who has known their wants and weaknesses and transgressions, and is able and willing to sympathise with them. In all ages these needs have been felt, and it seems as if this sense of need had prepared men to welcome one who should appear with such pretensions. We may venture then to say, that, even apart from all authority, we have reason to believe that there exist in the Divine nature these personalities of Father and Son; and the light which this fact throws on the whole conception of the spiritual world, and of Man's place in it, and relation to it, shows us that the revelation of it is no superfluous information, but is of the highest importance in the moral and spiritual education of man. For this discovery of the Son seems to open to us the structure of the spiritual world; it helps us to understand its organisation, and to see that its unity arises out of the principle of trust or recipiency,—the loving, dependent recipiency of the Son.

The almighty and all-wise Father is the ocean-fountain in which all goodness is treasured up, that goodness being a righteous love which ever seeks to communicate itself; the Son receives out of the fulness of the Father, and communicates of that fulness to the whole spiritual creation. The spiritual creation constitutes the body of the Son, its countless individualities going to make up the organs and members of that body in all its fair proportions. For he is "the beginning of the creation of God," the point, so to speak, in the

Divine nature from which the creation proceeds. And as he is himself essentially the Truster, the Believer, the Receiver from his Father, so he is on that account the fit channel of the life and Spirit of God to the whole spiritual order; his presence in each individual of that order giving it its filial relation to the Father, and its consequent capacity of receiving out of the fulness of God.

It appears to me that the chief difficulty in the way of admitting the claim of Jesus of Nazareth to be the Son of God is surmounted when we have arrived at these conclusions. For surely if this revelation was to be made on earth at all, the place for it was the land of Judea, the land where dwelt that old Semitic tribe to which the true idea of God as a teaching Father had been given as an inheritance from the beginning. Where could that idea receive so fitly its culminating personal development as in the land where it had been so long guarded as a sacred deposit, and where, as it passed along the glorious line of patriarchs and lawgivers and psalmists and prophets, it was always associated with the prediction and expectation of One who was to be the seed of the woman, despised and rejected of men, but who nevertheless should finish transgression and make an end of sin, and bring in an everlasting righteousness, and be called the Mighty God, the Father of the Everlasting Age, the Prince of Peace.

Unquestionably also the personal character of Jesus gives a great support to the truth of the claim which he makes for himself. As we read these simple biographies of him, we instinctively feel that he was God-like, and when he makes it, we are certain he has no selfish end in view; the revelation of the Father and the accomplishment of his will in the salvation of men are his sole objects, so that there is absolutely nothing in him to turn him aside from truth. He is indeed so wise, so good, so pure, so holy, so perfectly calm and unexcited, at once so human and so free from every human frailty, so clothed moreover with that mysterious majesty which impressed all who came in contact with him—and which continues to impress ourselves—as the seal of God authenticating all that he said and did, that we seem to be shut in, by reason and conscience, by reverence and highest instinct, to accept the claim which he makes for himself to be the Son of God—the Lord and Saviour and Head of man. And it is indeed a claim which we may well accept with thankful joy ; for though at first sight it appears to be for himself alone, yet on examination it proves to be a claim on behalf of every human being to be the child of God.

III.

THE PURPOSE OF GOD.

When I endeavour to conceive what a true religion ought to be, it seems to me that it must consist mainly in an explanation of my own conscience and my own life: for it is through my conscience or spiritual sense that any intimations come to me that I have relations and duties and interests beyond this visible world; and it is in my life that I feel the continual battle going on between the claims of that higher order of things and the pressing demands of sense and selfishness. Now, when I attentively consider what is going on in my conscience, the chief thing forced on my notice is that I find myself face to face with a purpose—not my own, for I am often conscious of resisting it—but which dominates me, and makes itself felt as ever present, as the very root and reason of my being. If it be objected that this consciousness is a mere result of education, and that the uneducated man has it not, I answer, Education, it is true, is required to develop or *educe* it, but does not implant it any more than it implants a capacity for music. Had I grown up without mental culture the thought might not have suggested itself to me, but when it is suggested, I recognise it at once as a true description of the history of my highest being.

This consciousness of a purpose concerning me that I should be a good man—right, true, and unselfish—is the first firm footing I have in the region of religious thought; for I cannot dissociate the idea of a purpose from the idea of a Purposer, and I cannot but identify this Purposer with the Author of my being and the being of all things, and further, I cannot but regard His purpose towards me as the unmistakable indication of His own character. I am sure that He must be Himself what He calls on me to be; and if He is really good, I can trust myself and the universe in His hands.

This is my first true conception of God. So long as I draw my conception of Him from the works of creation alone, I think of Him as a Being of infinite power and skill, but I do not get near to Him; I do not apprehend the object He is aiming at in myself and in my race by placing us in this strange conflict, and surrounding us by all these wonderful works: I do not understand the meaning of human life, so full of varied interest, so full withal of apparent failure and real suffering. But when once I come to feel that God has a purpose to make me good, I can also apprehend that the events of life may be the education which He uses for this end; and the conviction that this is His desire is pressed on me through the action of my conscience, for I find Him there at every moment insisting that I should conform my will to His in thought, word, and deed.

In this endeavour to confirm my hold of a personal relation between God and man and of His personal dealings with man, I find myself helped by realising my own personal individuality. I belong to a race and nature comprehending all human beings, yet I feel myself to be different from them all, and to require a treatment and guidance special to myself. God sees and knows me as a work of His own hands, altogether distinct from all His other works. He intends me to fill a place which no other creature can fill, and is dealing with me in accordance with this special individuality. Thus I feel myself, as it were, alone with God. He only fully understands me, and He meets my need, according to His full understanding of me, by a course of circumstances chosen for my own personal education by His fatherly love and wisdom. It seems to me that He meets my actual condition at each successive moment, so that I do not feel as though I were put under a law in order to undergo a certain process, but as face to face continually with One who is watching every change that comes over my spirit as much as if He had nothing else to care for in the universe, and who varies His dealings with me in accordance with these changes. He is thus *my* God and Father as well as *our* God and Father; and the consciousness of my own personality seems necessarily to involve belief of *His* personality.

In saying I believe that God has created me with the purpose of training me into the participation of His own righteousness, I only say what I am sure every one who attentively considers the meaning of the voice of conscience within him must agree with. Evidently He whose presence that voice indicates is most earnest that we should be righteous. I am sure of this, notwithstanding all the difficulties arising out of the actual circumstances of life.

The fact also that man possesses capacities both moral and intellectual which require development seems to suggest that education must have been the purpose of his creation, however much there may be in the spectacle of the world around us making this very difficult of belief. There is indeed but small appearance there of anything like a divine purpose of education. The capacities of human beings can only be rightly or fully developed in what may be called fortunate or favourable circumstances, yet when we look around we see many—indeed, the majority of human beings—placed in circumstances which appear most adverse to anything like moral culture. What can we say of the educational prospects of the populations outside of the Christian pale, or even of the greater number of those within it? What can be said of the lanes and closes of our own large towns, but that they seem fitter to train men in vice and profligacy than in spiritual goodness? The great masses of the population appear to have their mental and moral capacities overpowered by the pressure of physical want or the craving for sensual gratification, and of those who are raised above this abject condition how many are taken up with merely selfish pursuits, with the desire to procure wealth or power or pleasure or ease!

Such facts are strange enough, and in the face of them I could hardly adhere to the belief that there is really a divine purpose of love brooding over these strange scenes, did I not also believe that there is no haste with God. The fact moreover of the existence of a moral sense within man, which makes him always feel that he ought to be better than he is, outweighs to my reason all these difficulties. This moral sense is certainly the distinguishing and characteristic feature of humanity, clearly indicating the purpose of the Creator that it should finally modify and control the whole man. And surely we ought not to judge of God's purposes by what we actually see accomplished in man, so much as by the indications given in the potentialities and capacities which have been bestowed on him, and which in their development may change the whole state of things. We are evidently in the midst of a process, and the slowness of God's processes in the material world prepares us, or ought to prepare us, for something analogous in the moral world; so that at least we may be allowed to trust that He who has taken untold ages for the formation of a bit of old red sandstone may not be limited to threescore years and ten for the perfecting of a human spirit.

I am satisfied that the moral sense which my Creator has placed within me must indicate His own character. He must Himself possess that righteousness which He calls for in me. And if so, is He not calling for *sympathy* when He calls for righteousness? And may I not therefore feel assured that it is *Love* which has given me my being, and that the purpose of my loving Creator must be to make me capable of knowing His love and of returning it?

I feel that I am continually thwarting His purpose concerning me, and yet that He never ceases urging it. What is the meaning of this urgency? It is evidently the urgency of One who desires that I should sympathise with Him,—that I should think and feel as He does; and what can it be but love that thus desires sympathy? The God who is Love cannot allow me to separate myself from Him. He is a jealous God, marking and condemning every obliquity, but only with the purpose of delivering from it; and when I understand His meaning my desire will always be according to that right prayer, "Search me, O Lord, and know my heart; try me, and know my thoughts; and see if there be any wicked way in me, and lead me in the way everlasting.'

The assurance that the righteous Creator can never cease to desire and urge the righteousness of His creature is the eternal hope for man, and the secure rest for the soul that apprehends it. For if this be His purpose for one, it must be His purpose for all. I believe that it is His purpose for all, and that He will persevere in it until it is accomplished in all.

When I speak of education, let me not be supposed to mean merely the progressive development of the race through successive generations. I mean the education of every individual of the race. Historically it is not always true that successive generations improve upon each other. We often find them not only stationary but retrogressive. If we regard God as caring only for the progress of the race, and not also and primarily for the progress and perfecting of the individuals who compose it, we lose the idea of His fatherly relation to man. Such an interest would be the æsthetic interest of an artist in his work, not that of a father in his children. Unless the individual be immortal there can be no religion for man. On this condition alone can we believe in God's fatherly love, or even—if it be possible to distinguish between them—in His righteousness. I shrink from the argument that, because on a fair calculation of the comparative good and evil of our brief span here the good is found rather to preponderate, we are therefore bound in reason to be thankful for the gift of life, even on the supposition that there is no hereafter for us. The capacity of discerning the excellency of goodness, and of apprehending that there must be an infinitely good and blessed God, gives a hope, which we are justified in interpreting as a *promise* from God, of a life that shall not end for every human being.

Yet neither in this state nor in any other are men intended to be a mere mass of units; distinct as is the idiosyncrasy of each and individual as is the training required by each, they are intended to constitute an infinitely varied and complicated, yet orderly, whole; that is, to be members of a body in which each may fill a place for which he is specially fitted, and to supply a want which could not otherwise be supplied. And therefore, although I believe that the education of the individual is God's primary purpose for him, yet I also believe that the ultimate object of education is to fit him for his place in the spiritual society. With the human body as our type, we perceive how varied are the uses for which the different members are intended, and consequently how varied must be the training necessary for their development. And when along with this almost infinite diversity of training we take into account the power of resistance which the human will may oppose to any process of discipline, we see how the period of training may be indefinitely lengthened out.

If this be so, is it a correct description of man's state in this world to call it a state of Probation? Are we placed here only to be *tested* and *proved* whether we will walk in God's ways or in our own ways? Has God created us merely that He might see what we would do—how we would use the talents and opportunities given to us? Does He say, "I have given you a certain amount of light and certain powers of using that light, and I will see whether you are faithful to this trust, and if not I will cast you off;" and does He conclude this warning by saying, "Be diligent, for the time of probation is limited to the present life; at its close the judgment will take place, and the everlasting award will be given"?[1] Is this, I repeat, a full account of

[1] See Ps. lxxvii. 7-10: "Will the Lord cast off for ever?

our condition here? Most assuredly our lives are composed of trials, at every step good and evil are set before us and we are called to choose between them, and we are conscious that a judgment is passed upon us in every case according as our choice is right or wrong. It would be folly to deny this, or even to question it. I do neither, but I ask whether God has not a purpose to serve by all this trial beyond that of merely testing us? And if He has, ought not the whole process to take its name from that purpose rather than from the means by which it is attained?

What then can we suppose His purpose to be? Is it not the development of all our capacities? Is it not, in a word, education? Is He not saying to us, I have created you to be My children—partakers of My own spirit—of My own righteousness—of My own blessedness,—and I have given you capacities conformable to this high calling, capacities of apprehending Me and My purposes, and of

---

Will He be favourable no more? Is His mercy clean gone for ever? doth His promise fail for evermore? Hath God forgotten to be gracious? hath He in anger shut up His tender mercies? And I said, This is my infirmity: but I will remember the years of the right hand of the Most High."

becoming fellow-workers with Me in carrying them out ?[1]

I contend that the revelation of God as the Father necessarily involves the belief that education is the purpose with which He created us, and that probation must always be subservient to that end, and can never be itself the end. No education can go on without trial; but *we are tried that we may be educated, not educated that we may be tried.*

It is manifest that these two views of human life are in principle opposed to each other, and lead to opposing conceptions of the character of God and of the relation in which we stand to Him. The essential characteristic of a father's love is that it is inextinguishable. If I believe in God as the righteous Father, whose one purpose in all His dealings with man is to train him into a participation of His own righteousness that he may thus be a partaker in His blessedness, I cannot but trust

[1] See Deuteronomy xxx. 14, 15, 20: " The word is very nigh unto thee, in thy mouth, and in thy heart, that thou mayest do it. See, I have set before thee this day life and good, and death and evil ; . . . that thou mayest love the Lord thy God, that thou mayest obey His voice, and that thou mayest cleave unto Him : for He is thy life."

Him, and feel myself safe in His hands, eternally safe; and this trust opens my whole being to Him, and is thus essentially the only righteousness which a creature can have.

On the other hand, if the paramount relation of God towards us be that of a Judge—I should say that trust in Him becomes impossible. The justice of a judge consists in the unswerving integrity with which he discharges the duties of his office, uncorrupted by bribes and unmoved by either threats or entreaties. He must take part neither with nor against the offender; he must silence any feeling either of love or enmity, and simply desire that the law may have its course. He has not to consider what effect the execution of the sentence may have upon the character of the accused; all he has to do is to take care that it is the sentence decreed by the law. Any confidence therefore that I can have in the award of a righteous judge is in fact a confidence in myself—a confidence that I have right on my side, and that it would be unrighteous to condemn me. But in very truth I have no such confidence. I am conscious of many sins and shortcomings. I know that I have not right on my side, and that an impartial award on the merits of my case must be condemnatory. If therefore I come to the conclusion that I am here simply on trial, if I regard God as One who is keeping, as it were, a debtor and creditor account with me, and who will deal with me according to that account, I may in word call Him Father and in word ascribe love to Him, but I cannot really regard Him as a Father, nor trust in His love, nor feel myself safe in His hands.

This idea of probation corresponds exactly to the idea of Law which occupies so large a space in the epistles of St. Paul, and which is by him contrasted with the idea of Gospel. It narrows our conception of all we have to look for from God to strict impartiality; so that any hope of a favourable judgment from Him must necessarily rest on the estimate we form of our own obedience— our own conformity to the standard of the law. And when the truth is at last forced upon us that the law requires nothing short of unselfish love to God and man, in thought, word, and deed, all hope founded on obedience is utterly swept away, because we discover that we have not only in time past been living in neglect of this great commandment, but that we never can obey it by any efforts in our power. We are thus shut up into hopeless condemnation both as regards the past and the future. Evidently in such circumstances we can find no help from the character of God; it is a mere terror to us, making filial trust absolutely impossible. On the principle of Law there is no place for forgiveness, and when we become conscious of having sinned we see no outlet from condemnation. This is our inevitable condition so long as we believe ourselves to be in "a state of probation." We have no hope in ourselves, for we feel that we are sinners; and we have no hope in God, for we see in Him only an impartial retributive justice.

"But," it will be said, "you are leaving out of sight the Gospel. The supreme Judge desires mercy if it can be reconciled with justice, and He himself has devised the means. His Son has taken on him the nature of the sinful race, and consents to undergo the penalty due to sinners; they are forgiven on the condition of believing in their Redeemer, and thus mercy has its free course, and yet justice is inviolate."

The errors which I conceive to be involved in this statement have been elsewhere dealt with.[1] Here I would only say that so long as the idea of probation is retained, it robs even the Gospel of its healing virtue, suggesting, as it does, that this revelation brings no unconditional blessing but only varies the form of our trial,—the final award being now suspended, not indeed on perfect obedience, but on the answer to the question, Are you a believer? thus forcing us to seek our confidence, not in the Father's forgiving love revealed in the gift of His Son, but in our performance of the task of believing; an undefinable task which no man, whilst thus contemplating it, ever knows whether he has accomplished or not.

Other evils of no small moment result from this view. Among the most perilous are these : that it almost necessitates a self-justifying spirit, and that it suggests the wish that the standard of righteousness were lowered. Then again, it tends to make us more occupied with the

[1] See the Chapter which treats of Propitiation, *et passim*.

consequences of sin than with its moral evil—with the thought how we may escape punishment, rather than with the hope of becoming righteous. Hence also the life and death of Christ have come to be regarded rather as a propitiation to Divine justice through which mercy may be extended to the guilty, than as a manifestation of that righteousness which God desires to see in us, and of His own righteous love, which, whilst it never ceases to condemn our sin, can never cease to seek our deliverance from sin.

We may conclude then that the conception of our relation to God, as interpreted by the idea of probation, is actually opposed to the spirit of Christianity; for there is nothing in it which answers to the announcement that God is the loving Father of all men; nothing therefore which can help us to flee to Him and to trust Him under a sense of weariness and weakness, of sorrow and suffering; nothing which can really help us to be righteous with the righteousness of filial trust.

If, on the other hand, we consider ourselves as created for the purpose of being educated into fellowship with God, and as ever living under the action of this purpose, the darkness passes away and all becomes light. We are no longer under the cold eye of a Judge, but under the loving and encouraging eye of a Father, who "willeth not the death of a sinner, but that he should turn from his wickedness and live;" and the assurance of daily forgiveness, as well as the blotting out of all past offences, imparts its own loving character to all the circumstances of our lot, and even to the punishments and sufferings which our Father sees fit to send. "He afflicteth not willingly, but for our profit; that we may be partakers of His holiness." The belief that this is indeed God's purpose is a continual call and help towards growth in righteousness, because it is fitted to inspire that inextinguishable trust in Him which is itself the *right* state of the creature. I would say, then, that this idea of the purpose of our Creator is the very basis of all true thoughts of Him and of our relation to Him. Without it Christianity ceases to be a gospel; it loses its fundamental meaning: for the Gospel of Christ is in very deed the manifestation of this purpose and of the way in which it is to be accomplished.

E

But whilst we reject this false conception of the Divine purpose, do we mean to say that man can ever over-estimate God's hatred of evil? Assuredly not. The error consists, not in exaggerating His condemnation of sin, but in not perceiving that under this condemnation lies an unchanging purpose to deliver us from it. I would even say that the man who regards God simply as a just judge, and who is by that consideration urged to a continual effort after righteousness (though it is certain that whilst ignoring God's fatherly relation to him he never can attain to righteousness and must be always in unrest) is doubtless in a higher moral condition than the man who allows his idea of God's fatherly love to lower his idea of God's holiness and abhorrence of sin. Moreover in the former case an experience of the futility of mere effort to fulfil the law of love may lead to the discovery that filial trust is the only spirit in which the fulfilment of that law is possible. In this way the law may be a schoolmaster to lead him to Christ, by shutting up every other path and showing him that it can only be fulfilled in the heart which regards God as a loving and forgiving Father.

Self-trust is manifestly the principle inherent in that false conception of the law, according to which our hope before God depends on our obedience to its requirements; and self-trust is the root of all sin, being the substitution of self for God. The belief that we are under a process of education, through which it is God's purpose to train us into righteousness, at once sets us free from this bondage, by leading us to cast ourselves upon that loving purpose as a refuge from all the evils which we feel within us, and to see in its unchangeableness a security for its ultimate triumph over everything which opposes it.

It is a memorable moment in the history of a man's spirit when the righteousness of God ceases to be a ground of anxiety or apprehension and becomes a ground of assured hope and confidence,—when he perceives that it cannot be satisfied with punishment but must always desire to communicate itself. As soon as he discovers that the purpose of God in giving him a law is to train him into a participation of His own righteousness and blessedness, that very moment the Law becomes Gospel and his Judge becomes his Father. The revelation of this purpose then is the Gospel, and it is virtually made to every man, for the light in his conscience which condemns his sin ought to be understood as "the goodness of God leading him to repentance." What means God may use for this end we cannot tell, but when we see what His fatherly purpose is we are enabled to trust ourselves in His hands and to look without fear into an unending futurity. We can rest in the assurance that the only power in the universe—the power by which all other things exist—seeks and must ever seek for us that righteousness which is our only possible blessedness.

But, it may be asked, is it possible to reconcile the aspect of the world with the existence of such a purpose? How are we to judge of the purpose of God but by what we actually see taking place under His government? When we see the evil everywhere so far exceeding the good, are we justified in believing that He really condemns and abhors evil, or that He really has the purpose of educating all men into fellowship with Himself?

There is an answer to these questions which fully satisfies my reason, and it is this: I am conscious in my own inner man of an overshadowing of evil, just as I see it in the outer world; but I am also most distinctly conscious of the Divine condemnation resting upon it all, and of a call on me to take part with God in His condemnation of it and His conflict with it. I am sure that this is the true account of the world within me, and I am constrained by reason and conscience to interpret by it the state of the world without me. I am sure that the condemnation of God rests on all sin there too, however unchecked it may seem to be, and I am also sure that this same witness of God against all evil, which I feel within myself, is really in the heart of every human being, unheard and unattended to though it may be; and I cannot otherwise interpret this witness than as the expression of God's purpose of unchanging love, which will never cease its striving till it has engaged every child of man to take part with Him in this contest.

In coming to this conclusion, it is manifest that I am constrained to adopt the assurance that this purpose follows man out from his present life, through all stages of being that lie before him, unto its full accomplishment. And indeed unless we accept this assurance, we must give up the idea that the purpose of God in creating man was to educate him, for no otherwise can it be maintained. But verily it seems to me that in giving up this idea we are actually giving up the idea of God altogether, and surrendering ourselves to atheism as well as despair. For what is true theism but the belief that the ruling Power in the universe, the only absolute Power that exists or can exist in space or in duration, is a Being whose nature is righteous love, who is therefore the enemy of all sin, and who will never cease His endeavours to extinguish it, and to establish righteousness throughout His moral creation?

To me it appears that there can be no real gospel, no real good news for man, which does not involve this assurance. In point of fact, no one who believes in a righteous God at all can conceive the possibility of His ever ceasing to condemn sin; and surely His condemnation of our sin necessarily implies His demand for our righteousness, just as the condemnation of darkness necessarily implies a demand for light. This has not been sufficiently considered by theologians, who have generally represented the holiness of God as an attribute rather fitted to quench the hopes of a sinner than to encourage them;[1] although it is the very attribute in which the old prophet Habakkuk first seems to have found a light and a power, enabling him to realise for himself and his countrymen that the purpose of God in sending affliction is not to *destroy* but to *correct*,—that is, to educate. "Art Thou not from everlasting, O Lord my God, mine Holy One? we shall not die. O Lord, Thou hast ordained them for judgment; and, O mighty God, Thou hast established them for correction" (Hab. i. 12).

Those who conceive of justice as opposed to mercy must regard the Psalmist's utterance, "Also unto Thee, O Lord, belongeth mercy, *for* Thou renderest to every man according to his work" (Ps. lxii. 12), as a complete subversion of the meaning of words, and I have sometimes thought they must be tempted to conjecture that the copyist has by mistake substituted the word *mercy* for *justice*. They

---

[1] "Sing unto the Lord, O ye saints of His, and give thanks at the remembrance of His holiness."—Ps. xxx. 4.

have been accustomed to suppose that nothing worse could befall them than that God should render unto them according to their works, and their hope in His mercy has just been the hope that He would not so deal with *them;* the idea therefore that mercy itself will render unto them according to their works seems to be the annihilation of all hope.

I believe that all this is founded on misapprehension, and that in God mercy and justice are one and the same thing,—that His justice never demands punishment for its own sake, and can be satisfied with nothing but righteousness, and that His mercy seeks the highest good of man, which certainly is righteousness, and will therefore use any means, however painful, to produce it in him. If men could understand that God's purpose in rendering to them according to their works is to instruct them in the true nature and character of their works, that so they may apprehend the eternal connection between sin and misery, between righteousness and blessedness, and thus be led to flee from sin and take hold of righteousness, they would also understand that it is in mercy that He deals thus with them, and that in fact the purposes of mercy can in no other way be accomplished.

I know that I should be a minister of good to many if I could help them to apprehend that this is the meaning of God's justice, and therefore that it is to be as much trusted in as His mercy. They have been accustomed to look upon Christ as their Saviour because he has delivered them from justice by suffering the penalty which it denounced against them, whilst in truth he is their Saviour by revealing to them that justice is their friend, being only the enemy of their enemy.

The purpose of God, whether He punishes the sinner or remits the punishment, is always the merciful one of delivering him from sin, not that of carrying out the principle of retribution. The awful amount of misery which we see in this world proves that He will not shrink through false tenderness from inflicting any suffering which He knows to be needful, but the conviction that His one purpose through it all is to draw the sinner out of sin into righteousness, enables us to contemplate Him through it all as a righteous Father.

We *are* by virtue of God's will and purpose

in the relation of children, and are therefore not called on to make ourselves children, but, in the knowledge of a relationship which already exists, to yield ourselves to our Father's instruction that we may become His righteous children. The sonship is not a new relation communicated through faith [or any other subjective means], but is itself coeval with man's creation; and although those on whom it was bestowed have forgotten it and have wandered from their Father's house into a far country, yet when they there learn to know the evil of their ways and remember that they have a Father, because they *are* sons God sends forth the Spirit of the Son into their hearts, crying, "Abba, Father." The same thing is taught by our Lord when, after exhorting his disciples to love their enemies and to do good to them that hate them, he uses this argument: "that *ye may be*—that is, *become* ($\gamma \acute{\epsilon} \nu \eta \sigma \theta \epsilon$)—the children of your Father which is in heaven." He assumes that God *is* their Father, and calls on them, not to *make* themselves His children, but *to be* His children; in other words, to walk worthy of their high relationship, as we say to the degenerate son of a good human father—Be your father's son.

The belief that we have been created for education affords, I am convinced, the only explanation of the endless varieties of human life—the only approach to the solution of its mystery. This principle I regard as the very basis of the Gospel; proclaiming, as it does, God's eternal and unchanging purpose for man, to raise him by education into fellowship with Himself, to make him a partaker in His own righteousness and His own blessedness.

IV.

THE BIBLE IN RELATION TO FAITH.

When we contemplate the attitude which criticism, historical and scientific, has now assumed in relation to the books of Scripture, we must feel that it is the duty of all who have been accustomed to regard the doctrine contained in these books as a reality of inestimable value, to consider whether in the face of this criticism, and allowing it everything which it may justly claim, they can yet hold Christianity in its entireness, and feel justified both in reason and conscience whilst they do so.

We know well that there are many truly good people who think that they hold their religion simply and in the last resort on the authority of the Bible, and that anything which weakens that authority, even on matters which have nothing to do with doctrine—such for example as natural history—must therefore be an evil thing, tending to rob men of all hope in God. They have accepted it as a principle, that the importance of every word of the Scriptures rests on the same ground, namely that the book is divinely and supernaturally inspired; any doubt therefore cast on the accuracy of its statements, in any matter whatsoever, seems to shake the whole of their religious faith; for they imagine that if that ground were to give way in the smallest matter, it would really give way entirely.

It is misapprehension like this that has given so terrible an interest to "*Essays and Reviews*" and to Bishop Colenso's "*Critical Inquiries into the Structure of the Pentateuch;*" and, so far as it prevails, every one, who feels the value of the truths contained in the Bible, must look on all such works with trembling jealousy and horror. Is there any valid and unshakeable protection against the fears thus stirred up? and if there be, what is it? This seems to me to be the great question for our time, which must be answered before there can be, for a large portion of our people, any true peace, or any firm standing-ground for their faith.

We all feel the immense difference that there is between believing a principle of reason or morals because we apprehend its necessary truth, and accepting it because some person in whose veracity and intelligence we have confidence has announced it. In the first case we are actually believing in the principle, in the second our faith is only in the veracity of our informant. The importance of this distinction is thoroughly recognised in every other department of knowledge. In that of religion it certainly is not generally recognised, and that for various causes. In the first place it seems more reverent to receive Divine truth simply on authority. The authority which Protestants acknowledge is that of a book which they regard as divinely inspired for the very purpose of communicating to men information as to the things of God which they could not otherwise possess. To use their finite reason therefore in judging of the contents of the book they are disposed to consider a presumptuous and irreverent denial of the necessity of such a revelation.

A second cause is to be found in misconception as to the nature of faith, which has been in some quarters strangely enough imagined to be opposed to knowledge, and has thus been lowered into a test and exercise of blind unquestioning obedience, instead of being regarded as the spiritual faculty which may perceive and receive Divine truth, from whatever source it comes. This may in some measure account for the idea that there is irreverence in presuming to expect to know anything of God except on outward authority. The expectation seems like undervaluing, if not setting aside, the Bible. Now I do not say that man could, without an external revelation, have arrived at that knowledge of God which is communicated in the Scriptures, —for indeed the history of the efforts of the human mind contradicts such a thought—but that after the communication has been made he can perceive its coherency and reasonableness, even to the length of seeing that it *must* be so and could not be otherwise, and that though he owes his first sight of Divine truth to the outward authority he may come to hold it as a possession of which no questioning or shaking of the outward authority can rob him.

I have often imagined to myself the large joy which must have filled the mind of an Aristarchus of Samos when the true conception of the solar system first dawned upon him, unsupported though it was by any of the mathematical demonstrations which have since convinced all educated men of its truth, and constraining belief solely on the ground of its own simple and beautiful order. I could suppose such a belief very strong and almost taking such a form as this : It is so harmonious, so self-consistent, that it *ought* to be so, therefore it *must* be so. And surely this is nothing more than might be looked for in regard to spiritual realities. If man is created for fellowship with God there must exist within him, notwithstanding all the ravages of sin, capacities which will recognise the light and life of the eternal truth when brought close to him. Without such capacities revelation would in fact be impossible. Where a Divine communication is bestowed, a fitness to receive it must exist, otherwise it could be of no use. Just as the eye can discern—though it cannot create —light, and without the eye light would be useless. I am not more sure of my own existence than I am of being under the eye and guidance of a Being who desires to train and educate me to be a good man; and yet I know that beyond the pale of the Bible's influence this conviction has rarely been fully felt, and I well believe that without that influence I should not have had such a conviction. But now that by the help of the Bible I have arrived at it, I feel that no demolition of outward authority, even if such demolition were possible, could deprive me of it. Indeed that agreement between the Bible and my spiritual organisation strengthens my faith in the Divine origin of the Bible more than any other argument could.

When I ask myself what reason or right I have to believe that the great Being who made and orders all things really cares for men and has a purpose of good for them in all the circumstances of their lot, it is not enough to answer that I have read this in a very ancient book, or been taught it by a venerable Church. There are objections to such belief which require a more thorough answer; I must myself see and handle its truth. And when I carry my questioning a little further, and ask myself what reason or right I have to believe that a man who lived in Palestine 1860 years ago was the Son of God, in order to be certain that in this belief I have hold of a substance and not of a mere shadow, I must discern in the history itself a light and truth which will meet the demands both of my reason and conscience. In fact, however true the history may be, it cannot be of any moral or spiritual benefit to me until I apprehend its truth and meaning. This and nothing less than this is what I require, not only in this great concern but in all others; for the only real instruction is that which helps us to perceive the truth and meaning of things, not that which merely asserts that such and such things are true and insists on our accepting them as such.

It has been the chief aim of my life to possess such an apprehension of the truth of Christianity as this; and it is now forty-five years since I ventured to give through the press an utterance to this desire, and to accompany it with a sketch of the meagre progress I had then made in realising it. I was brought up from my childhood in the belief of the supernatural and miraculous in connection with religion, especially in connection with the person and life and teaching of Jesus Christ; and like many in the present day I came, in after life, to have misgivings as to the credibility of this wonderful history. But the patient study of the narrative and of its place in the history of the world, and the perception of a light in it which entirely satisfied my reason and conscience, finally overcame these misgivings and forced on me the conviction of its truth. A good deal of this cannot perhaps be fully communicated to others, but, of that which can, I wish to record as distinctly as I am able what, having found helpful to myself, I think may perhaps be helpful to them.

The Bible assumes that we have some innate original capacity of apprehending spiritual truths when revealed, and to this capacity it addresses itself, that we may find God and know Him for ourselves; and until we do thus know Him it has not for us accomplished the only object for which it can have been given. It addresses the spiritual capacity, just as Kepler and Newton in their exposition of the laws of the material world addressed the intellectual capacity. And as the discoveries of these philosophers are now accepted, not on the personal authority of the discoverers but on the ground of their own discerned truth, so no man who has discerned the truth of the spiritual discoveries contained in the Bible continues to rest his faith on the outward authority of the book, but has an assurance of them—grounded on his own discernment of their truth, that is, their agreement with the inward facts of his spiritual consciousness and with the outward facts of his life—as firm as he has of his own existence. Although he would never have come to know them without this communication from without and from above himself, yet when he does know them it is their own discerned truth, and not the authority of their vehicle, which makes them objects of faith to him.

If we cannot have a firm apprehension and conviction of God's character and of His relation to ourselves in His Son, except in so far as we are assured that the book which contains a declaration of these eternal facts is directly and supernaturally inspired, I can see no hope of any satisfactory escape from the perplexities into which we have fallen; for on this supposition I cannot see how any indisputable evidence of such inspiration is attainable. But I believe that we may have such an apprehension, because the intrinsic necessary truth of these facts may be discerned, and I also believe that on this discernment our faith in the authority of the Bible must ultimately rest.[1]

It may be asked, "Are you giving to God the honour due to Him when you insist on seeing the rightness and reasonableness of a doctrine before you consent to receive it? Would it not be more reverential, more in accordance with the modesty becoming a crea-

---

[1] The most zealous defenders of the verbal inspiration of the Bible admit that there are parts of it of less importance than others. This is a great admission, because another is involved in it, namely that we ourselves must be judges of the comparative importance of these different parts. We cannot escape this responsibility and we cannot define or limit it. The 13th chapter of Deuteronomy contains a remarkable acknowledgment of, and appeal to, the spiritual apprehension of the Jewish people. It supposes that a prophet is proclaiming a false religion, and that a miracle has been wrought in support of it, and it holds the people responsible for discerning and detecting the false religion, and rejecting the sign or wonder. There are many such appeals to our spiritual discernment in the Bible.

ture, to accept it without question on His bare word?" I know that many earnest Christians will make this objection; and I should wish to let them understand that I most heartily sympathise with the feeling which leads them to make it, although I think the feeling misplaced. If an earthly father desired to have his son's co-operation in some matter involving his own character, and had taken pains to explain to him the principle on which he had undertaken it, would he not feel disappointed were the son to say, "You need not explain your motives and the reasonableness of your conduct, your bare authority is sufficient for me"? I have supposed that the father wished his son's sympathy as well as his co-operation, and as he could not give sympathy without understanding his father's motives, would he not be actually frustrating his father's whole purpose by this misplaced obsequiousness? It is evident that no principles whatever, whether religious, moral, or social, can really be believed unless their truth is apprehended. Could any one, for instance, be said to believe in the doctrine of Butler's Analogy if he did not himself apprehend the truth of its principles?

I do not then say that a man *ought* to claim for himself the right of rejecting Christianity until he discerns its truth, but that he *can* and actually does only believe it in so far as his spiritual understanding apprehends its truth.

I would say also that the very form and character of the Bible show that it is intended to be used rather as an instrument of education than to be quoted as an authority, and that it is given, not that we should be satisfied with a knowledge of its words as if its authority were an ultimate ground of belief, but in order that through it we may become acquainted with God Himself and with our own actual relations with Him as a living Being. So long as our faith in God rests solely on our belief that the Bible is inspired we have no real faith in Him at all. We do not know Him, we only know the Bible's account of Him.

But the capacities of the mass of mankind are as yet but little developed in this region of thought;—they must be educated for it, and it is evident that all education must at least begin with authority. Children cannot be taught without it, and ninety-nine out of every hundred are children in understanding. So after all, and notwithstanding all that has been said, the world must be taught on the principle of authority. What use is there then, it may be asked, for insisting on the danger of substituting authority for light, when so small a fraction of the race are capable of distinguishing the one from the other?

The use is this—that education will be a very different thing if, instead of regarding authority as the normal and permanent condition of knowledge and belief, the teacher uses it as only a stepping-stone to real knowledge, and constantly endeavours to induce his disciples to use the eyes of their own understanding and to draw them into what light they are capable of receiving. According to military discipline a soldier has nothing to do with the purpose of the orders he receives, nor with their wisdom: he has merely to understand what they are and to execute them. The light he has to look for is not in the nature of the command but in the authority of the officer who gives it. But if instead of a commander I have a teacher, whose object is not so much that things may be done, as that I may become wiser and better by doing them, then the light I have to look for is not in the authority of my teacher, but in the meaning of that which he enjoins. His business is to help me to understand the principles which he sets before me and to discern for myself their truth; it is in this respect quite different from that of the officer, whose duty is not to explain his orders but to enforce obedience to them. The soldier who questions or judges his commander's orders is guilty of a breach of duty; the disciple of Christianity would be defeating the whole object of his teacher if he did *not* question and judge; that is, if he did not seek to apprehend for himself the light and truth contained in the teaching. The officer and the teacher must not exchange parts, neither must the soldier and the disciple. If they do, it will be under penalty of confusion and defeat.

A teacher who supposes that doctrines are presented as exercises of submissive obedience, not to be understood but blindly reverenced, will consider it his duty to root and strengthen in the mind of the learner the idea that the essence of faith is humble acknowledgment of authority; and men trained in such a school can scarcely be expected to distinguish between

God's character and His institutions, between the spirit and the letter of the Bible. The true teacher on the contrary will always remember that his business is to awaken the reason and conscience, and to make his disciple feel that, until apprehended there, the truth is neither known nor believed.

In the foregoing observations I have made frequent appeals to the testimony of conscience, assuming that it is a guidance to us, both in forming our ideas of what the character of God is, and what the duties of men are. To such appeals I believe that many will answer: The value of conscience depends on circumstances, a wrong education necessarily conducts to erroneous judgments, and therefore the only safety is in an infallible guide. But how, I ask, are we, apart from conscience, to ascertain the infallibility of any guidance? And if we could, how are we to be sure that we have really apprehended its meaning?

It is in vain that we attempt to evade responsibility by casting ourselves upon authority; we must at any rate choose our authority, and be responsible for that choice. If I take a church as my guide, I must be prepared to answer to God and to my own conscience for doing so; if I take the Bible as my guide, I must in like manner be prepared to give a reason for this. Moreover I must remember that any guidance which does not quicken and strengthen my own personal conscious intercourse and sympathy with God is false and hurtful, seeing that this conscious spiritual sympathy with God in purpose and action is the sum and substance of all true religion. A guide who does not help me to see light for myself, either in a doctrine or in a course of action, and who offers his own guidance instead of light, is turning me away from God, whatever that guidance may be; for no outward conduct can in itself be righteous apart from the spiritual principle which inspires it. So long as a man receives his Christianity merely on the authority of a church or a book —so long as it has not commended itself to his higher reason and moral sense, or reached his inner consciousness—he has no real hold of Christianity, he is believing only in his church or his book. There may be the most absolute belief in the infallibility of a church or in the inspiration of the Bible, along with the most absolute unbelief in the doctrine taught by them, because the truth of the doctrine may be altogether undiscerned.

Two principles are involved in this view of Christianity: first, that it is not a creation of the human mind, as some have asserted, but an eternal reality—an actual existence in the spiritual world—as real as the physical facts revealed by Galileo or Newton; and secondly, that we have faculties capable of discerning this spiritual reality, *when revealed to us*, in the same way as we have faculties capable of apprehending physical realities. The Bible presents to our spiritual capacities their proper objects—the character of God, His relation to men, and His purposes towards them—and we then only receive the blessing which God intends for us in giving it to us when we apprehend those great things of which it speaks and discern their eternal necessary truth; in other words, when our spirit actually meets God and we find that He is indeed a Father.

I am sure that the Bible was not given to me that my knowledge of it might stand *instead of* my knowledge of God, nor was it given merely to help me to form an opinion about Him or to stimulate my imagination to form a picture of Him; it was given to help me to find Himself, and to know Him as a reality altogether independent of the book; as a man whom I have been seeking after is independent of the directory which guides me to his house. I do not perceive the real value of the Bible until I in this way become independent of it. I now know its truth, because I have been able to verify its exposition of God from what I have myself found in Him, and I can now understand it better, because I can compare its statements with the living original of which it is the copy; now also I am in a condition to hear discussions on the nature of its claims with perfect calmness, because I know that it reveals the living God, and am therefore certain that its intrinsic value can be but little affected by any decision that is come to on that subject. It is the truth of the revelation contained in the Bible which I must be assured of, and the assurance of its inspiration in the sense of verbal infallibility (in which sense the word is most generally understood) is not necessary for this, and would even be prejudicial were it to become the ground of my faith and so to stand between me and the actual personal discernment of its truth.

At the same time, in arriving at the assurance of its truth, I have got hold of an argument in favour of its Divine origin, which will not allow itself to be easily set aside. How is it that when Greeks and Romans, besides the less endowed and enlightened races, failed so much in their endeavours to know God and His relation to men, a small despised tribe of the old Semitic race did even from their very starting-point attain to a considerable measure of this knowledge? It is surely a remarkable fact, that the true idea of God's nature and character and relation to men, as accepted by all earnest thinkers who have believed in a personal God at all, has never been truly arrived at (at least on any large scale) except through that teaching which from the earliest time prevailed in the Jewish race, and which, having passed on through a long succession of lawgivers, judges, psalmists, and prophets, ever advancing into greater fulness and clearness of light, finally expanded into Christianity, receiving its perfect development in Jesus Christ.

However ignorant the authors of the sacred

books may have been of natural science, and however tinctured by the peculiarities of their age and country, still, in all that they say, they hold forth the conception of a God loving righteousness and hating wickedness, and seeking to induce men to do the same. I cannot regard this as accidental. Greeks and Romans, Egyptians, Persians, and Hindoos had exercised their minds in the search after God with very questionable success; whilst this despised, unphilosophical tribe seem from the first to have possessed this knowledge, not as a secret confined to the learned class but as the common inheritance of the nation, not as a discovery of their wise men but as a communication of God Himself to their fathers. When we meet with any gleams of divine light in the writings of other nations of antiquity, they seem to be the peculiar property of certain gifted individuals—a Socrates, a Plato, a Seneca; but the Hebrew knowledge was a national possession which belonged to their race, and which they traced up to the patriarchs of the human family. No doubt such men as Moses, David, Isaiah, and Jeremiah might by their personal genius give a special illustration to the well-known truth, as their natural endowments might give them a special fitness to deliver some message of threatening or exhortation or consolation in the ears of their fellow-countrymen; but still it was a message from the God whose name had come down to them from their remotest ancestors. In all their writings there is nothing like an idea thought out and elaborated by the human intellect; there is everywhere the recognition of a divine communication.

I felt it impossible to doubt that this remarkable history was the result of a special direction and purpose of God; and that He gave the Jewish nation that peculiar light and guidance, not for their own sakes merely or chiefly, but that through them light and spiritual guidance might be given to the world.[1] I cannot but believe that the instruction is inspired, and as for the history I do not feel that there is any vital difference between a *true*

---

[1] I am quite aware that many expressions might be quoted from the Bible which seem to limit and nationalise, so to speak, the character of God, but to those who are seeking to learn its real meaning, there will be no difficulty in explaining these expressions in perfect consistency with, and in subordination to, the great idea of the God and Father of our Lord Jesus Christ.

history of a Heaven-enlightened and Heaven-guided nation and an *inspired* history. The presence of a special Divine care and direction in the progress and life of the nation is the great fact which forces itself upon my belief when I compare their knowledge of spiritual things with that of the other nations. I do not therefore believe the things contained in the book because I know it to be inspired, but I believe in its inspiration, because I have proved the truth of the great things revealed in it, namely, the character of God and His relation to men, and because I have not found that true conceptions of these great realities have been attained by any of the human race without its help.

I have never met with any argument against the inspiration of the Bible which seemed to me of convincing weight; but whether it is inspired or not it certainly contains a revelation which no other book does, a history of God's direct and special dealings with a nation, and the individuals of that nation, which has no parallel in the world. The belief of its inspiration, and the belief of the special Divine guidance that presided over the whole history of the race from the call of Abraham to the destruction of Jerusalem are apt to melt into each other and appear like one belief, but they are two distinct beliefs, and the second appears to me to be by far the most important.

The whole literature of the country as connected with and influencing the spiritual education of the people was under this Divine guidance. In all the heathen religions the only unvarying attribute of God is power. In the Bible He is always the righteous Father, whose purpose is to educate men into a conformity with His own will, through a knowledge of Himself. To carry out this purpose He is represented as choosing a particular people, that in them He might exhibit the universal principles of His dealing with men. The *form* in which those principles are exhibited is exceptional, but the principles themselves are not exceptional. Our attention is attracted by the exceptional form, but the form is not itself the important thing; its use lies in revealing and drawing attention to principles which are quietly doing their work through the whole sphere of human nature.

As it seems to be God's purpose to educate

the individual through the conscience, so it seems His purpose to educate the conscience through this revelation. The conscience or moral reason, although it accepts the true idea of God, does not seem capable of originating it; revelation therefore is the needful complement of conscience, without which conscience is incomplete. Can we conceive that this incompleteness would be left unremedied? Ought we not rather to believe that He who has put His own light within every man has also, in this historic and living course of instruction, given a guidance by which that light may be rightly used?

V.

THOUGHTS ON ST. PAUL'S EPISTLE TO THE ROMANS.

It is scarcely conceivable that any one can be acquainted with the character of St. Paul, as delineated in the record of his life and in his own epistles, without loving and admiring him. He evidently belonged by his natural gifts and capacities to the highest type of man. He was a real hero, full of nobleness and yet full of tenderness—most impulsive and impetuous, yet reasonable and self-controlled—thoroughly and enthusiastically imbued with the old feelings and traditions of his nation, yet the loving brother of the whole human family.

"Spirits are not finely touched but for fine issues," and as He who made him destined him to be His chief instrument in carrying out the greatest issue that was ever committed to the hand of man, He gave him a corresponding mental endowment.

It seems generally agreed by the students of St. Paul, that the Epistle to the Romans is in some respects the most important of all his writings. It refers less than his other epistles to the passing circumstances of any church or individual, and more exclusively to the fundamental and permanent principles of Christianity. It has also more of the character of a sustained logical argument, setting out, as it appears to do, with the avowed purpose of explaining the nature of righteousness and its connection with or dependence on faith, and in some sort carrying out that purpose even to the end. Yet notwithstanding this appearance of logical reasoning, which naturally gives the expectation of great clearness, there can be no doubt that considerable indistinctness of apprehension as to its meaning has prevailed, and that great variety of opinion has existed and continues to exist through all branches of the Christian Church, both as to the main drift of its argument and also as to the connection of that argument with the subordinate topics and discussions introduced into it. Thus although justification by faith is admitted to be the great subject of the epistle, yet men are not agreed as to the meaning of the phrase. Whilst some have supposed that justification means the rectification of a man's spiritual and moral nature in relation to God and man, produced by a belief of God's fatherly purposes concerning all men, others have held that it does not refer to character at all but to position, and that the justified man is a man to whom righteousness is imputed in virtue of his connection with Christ, to whom he becomes united by faith, and who therefore, though not himself righteous, is treated by God as if he were so, for Christ's sake. We may say the same as to predestination and election, with this addition, that these subjects are not only felt to be in themselves inscrutably mysterious, but the place which they hold in the epistle, and their connection with the rest of the argument, and the reason of their introduction there at all, are difficulties generally regarded as most perplexing.

Further, the ultimate triumph of good over evil in the case of every individual, which to some thinkers appears to be prominently inculcated in this epistle as a doctrine of the first magnitude and most conducive to righteousness, is yet regarded, probably by a majority of earnest Christians, as not only unsupported by the Apostle's language but as actually immoral in its tendency and entirely opposed to the whole teaching of Christianity.

Doubtless the epistle is difficult, and no one who has endeavoured to follow out the connection, or even to find a grammatical and logical sequence in many of its passages, such as those in chapters i. 16, 17, and iii. 21-27, will deny the difficulty; and, as these passages are evidently the texts to the rest of the epistle, any uncertainty as to them must necessarily affect the meaning of the whole. Many commentators have taken in hand to explain it; and no doubt some light, though not an entirely satisfying light, has thus been thrown upon it, but even this has not penetrated the mass of readers, so that there is still ample room for endeavours to help them.

It is easier to conceive, than to adopt and to

hold, the proper attitude of mind in which to attempt the illustration of such a book. There are opposite dangers to be avoided: there is the danger of coming to the task with a mind stiffened by dogmatic theology and afraid of allowing the human reason to judge of divinely inspired thoughts and words, yet any one entering on it without great reverence and without feeling the moral obligation of keeping his interpretations within the limits of his author's language and in harmony with the general teaching of his other writings, would be manifestly unfit for the undertaking. The student ought ever to remember that his great business is to apprehend and follow out the Apostle's thought, and not merely to give a plausible explanation of his words. He ought to bring with him principles and convictions with which to compare his author's statements, that he may be able to judge reasonably and logically between the different meanings which the text will bear, and at the same time he must have habits of free thought, and be willing to keep his mind open to receive any new ray of light, even although that light may discover mistakes in his own cherished bygone conclusions. Neither the commentator nor the student must forget that the materials of all religious thought and feeling lie in our own consciousness and moral reason, and that we are not warranted in adopting any theory of religion until we have succeeded in reconciling it with that light which God has placed within us.

The Apostle knew that the gospel which he preached was true, not merely because it had been communicated to him by direct revelation from above, but because it had commended itself to the light within him, and had helped him to understand the contradictions and conflicts of his own inner being, and the relation in which he stood to God and to all outward events and things; it could have had no meaning for him apart from that inner being of his and those relations. In like manner the expounder of St. Paul, nay even his ordinary readers, are then only qualified for their work when they also make use of their moral consciousness, and persevere in requiring its concurrence, whilst endeavouring to follow out and unfold the Apostle's teaching. We have the same spiritual needs and instincts as he, and the same faculties, in kind if not in degree, and also the same materials from which to satisfy those needs and on which to exercise those faculties; and we cannot really benefit by his thoughts, nor even understand them, unless we ourselves *think* them, and apprehend how our own spiritual necessities are met by them; that is, in fact, unless we take our stand upon his standpoint, and see how far our own faculties, acting on the same materials and in the same direction, can honestly go along with him to his conclusions.

When we ask ourselves what righteousness is, we have some difficulty in giving an answer.[1] Our moral sense apprehends it, but when we attempt a definition we find that we are only using synonymous words. And yet we feel that our capacity of apprehending and possessing righteousness is the highest thing within us, connecting us with a spiritual order infinitely transcending the material universe and its laws. We feel that it stands above any idea of mere utility, taken even in its largest sense, although all true utility must depend upon it. We feel that what Hooker has so eloquently

[1] See Appendix C.

said of Law in general—" that her seat is the bosom of God, her voice the harmony of the universe"—is essentially true of the law of righteousness, and that in leaving its guidance we separate ourselves from the bosom of God and from the fellowship of the spiritual order, and inflict on ourselves a greater evil than the utmost amount of either physical or mental suffering, unconnected with sin, can bring upon us.

In the material world we see beautiful order maintained by the operation of the law of gravitation. Do we know of anything analogous to this in the world of mind? Our inner consciousness reveals to us the existence of a spiritual order to which we belong and of a spiritual law to which we owe obedience; a law which though it does not necessitate our conformity to it, fails not to reproach us for every transgression and makes us well aware that we are continually diverging from it. Conflicting attractions act upon us, distracting our own spirit and bringing us into collision with our fellow-creatures. We need a supreme gravitation which shall subdue all inferior attractions and enable us to keep our right place in relation to the whole system. The planet, as I have said, has no choice in the matter; its proper centre of attraction and its law of gravitation are irresistibly and unchangeably imposed upon it, whereas each one of us must choose his centre and cannot but be restless and miserable until he has made the right choice.

When we behold the beautiful order of the heavenly bodies we could almost envy their unbroken peace, and wish that we like them had a law imposed on us which would make aberrations impossible. But spiritual beings must arrive at rest by another way. We too must have a centre, but it cannot be imposed upon us as it is on the material creation; we must learn to discern it and choose it for ourselves. God is the true centre of the spiritual world; and as the relation of the planet to the sun may be said to embrace and govern its relations to all the subordinate parts of the system, so our relation to God embraces and governs all our other relations, and our rightness with Him ensures our rightness with them, as our unrightness with Him ensures our universal unrightness.

In what then does rightness with God consist? We may confidently say that the great object of St. Paul in his epistle to the Romans is to answer this question,—to explain the nature of true righteousness and the way of attaining it. We ought not therefore to suppose that when he speaks of righteousness—or justification—by faith, he means to set forth any special technical doctrine, but rather that he means generally to teach that a man's true righteousness must commence with and proceed from a just apprehension of the character of God and of the relation in which he stands to God, so that he is then, and then only, truly righteous when he is right in this relation.

Moreover St. Paul believed that man was created in Christ Jesus, and that his rightness therefore in relation to God can be nothing else than the rightness *of the Son*, that is, a filial trustfulness which accepts the whole will of God as the will of a loving Father; and consequently he teaches that the basis and root of all human righteousness must be the assurance that God is indeed our Father and can never cease to be so, that He loves us not because we are worthy of His love but because

He is our Father, and that His eternal purpose towards us is a purpose of infinite love, to draw us out of all our unworthiness into perfect filial trust, and so into perfect participation of His own righteousness and blessedness. We cannot have rightness with God unless we trust in Him, and we cannot have filial trust unless we have the assurance of His paternal love, that is, of an inextinguishable love which will not indeed withhold any needed punishment, but which no sin of ours can ever weary out or weaken, a love which seeks our righteousness, and which will persevere until its object is attained.

St. Paul starts with the purpose of explaining these principles, and this purpose will be found to reappear throughout the whole epistle, subordinating to itself even those passages which seem to be most excursive and digressive. And if this be so we are warranted in looking on the epistle as substantially and essentially a treatise on ethics, that is, an exposition of the principles which lead to a right moral state in man.

The belief that it is the purpose of God to draw all men to true righteousness, and that this purpose will most surely be accomplished in the case of every individual, was in the mind of St. Paul a most important help towards possessing the faith which justifies or makes a man righteous, and this for an obvious reason. He believed that man's righteousness consists in, or at least is produced by, absolute filial trust in the fatherly love of God, and he saw in this purpose the strongest demonstration of that love; he probably also thought that no one in whose mind there lurks even the shadow of a suspicion that he may some day, by the force of temptation, so separate himself from God as to be finally lost, can possibly maintain this perfect filial trust in Him.

Such a fear, if realised, would it is manifest effectually preclude trust, and therefore I believe that all who have attained to any degree of real righteousness are, in fact, whatever their professed creed in this respect may be, virtually delivered from its bondage. "There is no fear in love, but perfect love casteth out fear, because fear hath torment; he that feareth is not made perfect in love."[1]

[1] See also Rom. viii. 15-17, and Gal. iv. 6, 7.

Whilst a son believes that by his own misconduct he has alienated his father's heart and converted him into an enemy, he cannot be *right* with his father,—that is, he cannot possibly love him or trust himself in his hands, or have any of those feelings which it becomes a son to have. But if he discovers that he has been entirely misjudging his father and putting a wrong construction on his conduct, and that those acts which had appeared to him stern and unforgiving were really dictated by wise fatherly love, and if he comes at last to the full conviction that his true welfare and happiness are, as they had been all along and ever must be, his father's chief objects, then all is changed, his mistrust passes away, and he becomes *right* with his father. He is justified or set right with him through faith in his fatherly purpose. This I believe to be the meaning of justification by faith, and that it has been altogether misapprehended by those who have converted it into an artificial and very conventional dogma, according to which the holding of a creed gives a man a favourable standing with God. I believe that St. Paul really meant to express this judgment concerning it when he said that he was not ashamed of the gospel of Christ, because it was the power of God unto salvation to every one who believed it. It has this *power* in virtue of the revelation it makes of this *righteousness;* that is, in virtue of the revelation which it makes of the fatherly purpose of God towards mankind which, whenever it is believed, will set men right with Him and make them His trustful, obedient children.

The English word "faith," like its Greek equivalent (πίστις), has two meanings, *belief* and *trust.* St. Paul teaches that filial trust is itself righteousness, *i.e.* the right state of man in relation to God, but that he can only get into that right state by believing in the fatherly relation and fatherly trustworthiness of God. The value of the gospel consists in its containing—in the person and work of the Son—the revelation and the evidence of this fatherly relation and trustworthiness, and the importance of believing it arises out of its fitness to produce filial trust in those who do believe; for if what I believe does not produce in me filial trust, it does not work rightcousness, and therefore is not the power of God unto salvation.

There are many educated men who, if they spoke out their real sentiments, would acknowledge that when they hear the phrase "justification by faith" they are conscious of a mingled feeling of repugnance and contempt. They consider it as conventional cant, as the mere password of a religious sect, which substitutes a belief of certain empty dogmas in the place of true moral worth. And yet these same men, if they would devote a little earnest thought to the subject, might find that this despised phrase really indicates the foundation of all morality. If they would read the Acts of the Apostles so as to become acquainted with the history and character of Paul, the heroic apostle of the Gentiles and the great teacher of this doctrine, they would feel that what he so earnestly preached cannot possibly be conventional cant, but must be connected with some deep root of reason and truth in human nature. But they have made up their minds that Christianity with all its doctrines rests solely on divine authority, that faith only means implicit acknowledgment of that authority, and therefore that a man who insists on trying principles by reason and conscience must necessarily set aside both.

It might be somewhat startling to such persons to hear any one say that the first clear conception he had come to of this doctrine of justification by faith, was derived from the reported conversations of another heroic apostle to the Gentiles, whose name has escaped all suspicion of cant or conventionality amongst succeeding generations, although like Paul he was condemned by his contemporaries as a setter forth of strange gods. In the dialogue concerning Rhetoric Socrates is represented by Plato as discussing with Gorgias the meaning and value of his art. Gorgias explains that it consisted in such a knowledge of the use of words as would enable those who possessed it to secure to themselves a favourable judgment from any tribunal before which they might have to appear. Socrates puts the question whether the guilt or innocence of the party was a circumstance of any importance in the matter, to which Gorgias answers, that without art on either side the right would probably prevail, but that the excellence of his teaching lay in this, that even the supporter of a wrong cause—the criminal who deserved punishment—if he used that teaching skilfully, would come off victorious. Socrates then suggests the inquiry whether it is really for the advantage of a man who is guilty that he should escape unpunished,—whether, on the supposition that the laws are really good, that is, wisely framed for the right education of the people, it can possibly be profitable for any one to evade their proper operation, and whether it would not on the whole be the best course for a man to pursue when he felt himself guilty, to present himself to the judge and crave punishment; and further when he knew any of his friends to be in this position, whether it would not be the truest friendship to urge or even to constrain them to do the same.

There is exquisite humour in the proposal, but there is a deep principle contained in it which is at the root of all righteousness. To pursue such a course would be possible only on the condition of absolute faith in the rightness of the laws and in the beneficial working of the punishments awarded by them; but it is evident that no man could be in *perfect* accord with the laws of his country who was not prepared to follow out the proposal.

The absolute wisdom of any human government, either in the enactment of laws or in their execution, must always be doubtful; and therefore an undoubting acceptance of them and submission to them, as an education in righteousness, is not to be expected, and might not always be profitable. But if there be a God, if there be an infinitely wise Governor of the universe, His dealings with men must always be intended to constitute such an education, and any one who really believes in God, and who at the same time really desires righteousness, is then only acting in consistency with this desire, and also with the highest reason, when he commits himself in entire confidence to His guidance and fully accepts all His providential dealings. This confiding state is the *right* state for a man to be in, and the entire and detailed righteousness necessarily resulting from it would be most properly named " the righteousness of faith."

Certainly Socrates meant to teach that

man's truest wisdom was to commit himself unflinchingly, and without regard to present ease and comfort, to the instruction and guidance of a divine wisdom, if such could be found, which would never cease its endeavour to conduct him into true and permanent righteousness, that being the only possible true and permanent blessedness. He was well aware of the faults of Athenian laws and judges, but he accepted them as representatives and types of a more excellent way. He had within himself the consciousness of an infallible guidance, and knew that it was only by entire subjection of himself and all his selfish imaginations to it, that he could profit by its instructions. All must be right with him who can identify this guidance with the Ruler of the Universe. Doubtless Socrates made this identification, and found in it the assurance that the Ruler of the Universe was occupied with the purpose of making him righteous, an assurance which enabled him to welcome everything which befell him, and to look for divine light and instruction in all ; and thus he was *justified* or set right by that same faith which put St. Paul right also.

Chapter I.

If we apprehend that without filial trust our moral capacities can never be fully developed, we shall understand how St. Paul in writing to the converts at Rome at once seizes on this as the chief characteristic of Christianity; " I am not ashamed of the gospel concerning Christ, for it is the power of God unto *Salvation,*" that is, unto spiritual life—unto the highest and deepest morality—for *in him* is revealed this all-important filial trust as accessible to all men.

He is addressing persons who in that city which was then the world's centre of political power and moral influence, had been drawn together by the sound of the gospel, and desiring to communicate to them his own convictions of the evil of sin and the mighty efficacy of the spiritual leaven contained in the gospel which he anticipated would yet leaven the whole of humanity. It is "*the power of God,*" he says, "unto salvation to every one who believeth,"—it contains the divine dynamics— it is the spiritual lever whereby men may be lifted out of sin into righteousness. It is clear that this lifting out of sin into righteousness is the chief meaning here of the term " salvation," although deliverance from the results of sin is also included. He takes for granted that God is righteous, and starting from this ground he proceeds through the course of the epistle to teach that faith or filial trust in God—the faith of Jesus himself—is the right or righteous state for man. And if we consider that man's righteousness must be determined by the relations in which he stands to that spiritual cosmos or order to which he belongs, and moreover that God is not only the Head and Author of that cosmos, but also the one Fountain out of which all righteousness must flow, we shall be convinced that this is the truest description that could be given of human righteousness; first because trust in the righteous God must itself be righteous, and secondly because it puts man in a condition to receive the inflow of God's righteousness.

It was the purpose of God that as men are sons—in virtue of having been created in the Son—they should also be partakers of the Son's love and holiness and blessedness by becoming partakers in his "faith," that is, in his dependent recipient filial trust in the Father. This filial trust is the special attribute of the Son, and the call on us for such trust contains in it the assurance that we *are* sons, as we could not otherwise answer the call.[1] Our participation in this trust is our righteousness, being that which keeps us right with God and His order, maintaining spiritual life within us and holding the lower nature in due subordination to the higher. And as this trust is man's righteousness, when he ceases to exercise it he loses his righteousness and necessarily falls into disorder and anarchy.

It was in this fallen condition that Paul contemplated men, and the glory of the gospel in his eyes was that it contained a fitting remedy. They had lost trust in God, and in order to have it restored they

---

[1] We are not to make ourselves sons by exercising the trust, but to exercise it in the belief that we are already sons. The thought that we are to entitle ourselves to trust in God by any doings or efforts of our own is a deceiving thought which, though it may commend itself to the uninstructed conscience, can never produce real righteousness, being opposed to any true self-appreciation and to that spirit of dependence which is the filial spirit. In fact it is of the nature of sin, which consists essentially in that self-trust which separates the creature from its Creator.

needed to have an assurance that although they had destroyed themselves God had not abandoned them, but still looked on them as His children, and still retained His original purpose of making them partakers of His own righteousness and blessedness. The gospel of Jesus Christ was the declaration of that purpose in a form suited to their present circumstances. They were conscious that they were sinners, and this consciousness made the thought of God a terror to them; they knew they had deserved His wrath, and they knew not—or believed not—that in wrath He remembers mercy; hence they could not trust Him. Yet nothing but filial trust could pro duce righteousness; therefore unless it could be made plain both to their reason and to their conscience that there did exist in God a fatherly love which no amount of sin could extinguish, there was no righteousness possible for them. To make this demonstration —to prove that God's fatherly relation was not broken off by their transgressions—the well-beloved Son came forth from the bosom of the Father.

St. Paul begins the epistle by declaring his

own official separation to the service of the gospel, which he calls "the gospel of God concerning His Son, who was made of the seed of David according to the flesh, and declared to be the Son of God with power, according to the spirit of holiness, by the resurrection from the dead, Jesus Christ our Lord, by whom we have received grace and apostleship, for obedience to the faith," or, in order to bring men under the obedience of faith. He thus appears to assume that the purpose of the gospel was to bring man into a state of trustful obedience, or under the influence of trust in God; and that the preaching of it consisted in the setting forth of Jesus Christ, as the Son of God who had taken man's nature and had *in that nature* been raised from the dead, and had thus been declared to be the Son of God according to the spirit of holiness, *by the resurrection from the dead.*

He makes no comment on this statement concerning "the Son of God." He apparently takes it for granted that the Roman disciples had learnt its meaning, for he expresses his thankfulness that their "faith was spoken of throughout the whole world;" but we are entitled to infer that the coming of Christ into our nature, and his victory over death, and his resurrection from the grave as our Head, form the substance of that gospel which he had been set apart to proclaim, and of which in the 16th verse he declares, I am not ashamed of it, "for it is the power of God unto salvation, to the Jew first, and also to the Greek; for therein is the righteousness of God by faith"—that is, by *trust*—revealed for our belief (δικαιοσύνη γὰρ Θεοῦ ἐν αὐτῷ ἀποκαλύπτεται ἐκ πίστεως εἰς πίστιν), "as it is written, The just shall live by faith."

When we first come upon this passage we naturally expect to find in it light as to the meaning of the gospel, but when we have studied it carefully most of us will confess that it has not fulfilled our expectations. We might have expected St. Paul to enlarge on the love of God who had thus revealed Himself to us in the eternal Son, and who had by sending that Son into our nature, after we had destroyed ourselves by sin, given us the assurance that He not merely forgives us but that He still regards us as beloved children. We might have expected him to dwell on the resurrection of Christ—the Head of humanity—as the pledge of a triumph over death and "him who has the power of death, that is, the devil," in which all the race shall ultimately participate. This would have been intelligibly a gospel. Instead of this we only find words about the "righteousness of God," somewhat difficult to put a meaning on. The English rendering affords no help; the translators appear to have given up hope of finding any meaning whatever in it, and to have satisfied themselves with setting down English words which might in some sort correspond with the original. And even in doing this they have been careless, for they have rendered the same Greek preposition (ἐκ) in two different ways in the same verse—*from* faith in the one clause, and *by* faith in the other—when manifestly its use in the second instance was intended to govern and to explain its use in the first. It ought to have been rendered "The righteousness of God *by* faith is revealed *to* faith"—or, for belief—"as it is written, The just shall live *by* faith," or perhaps better thus—"The just-by-faith shall live." The man, *i.e.*

who has been *rightened* or set right by faith shall live (ὁ δὲ δίκαιος ἐκ πίστεως ζήσεται). As the words stand in our translation they give no indication of the connection between that " righteousness by," that is, proceeding out of " faith " which gives the gospel its dynamic power, and the words quoted from Habakkuk; although the whole force of the passage lies in this connection. The glory of the gospel, the apostle tells us, consists in its full revelation of that "righteousness by faith" which, the old prophet declared, is *life* to the man who possesses it.

There can be no doubt that the great difficulty of the passage lies in this very expression, " the righteousness of God *by faith.*" Does it mean the righteousness of God in Himself—that is, as manifested in His own character and actings?—and if so, how can it be by faith? or does it mean a righteousness in man produced by faith? and if this is the meaning, why is it called the righteousness of God? and 'how can it be the distinguishing feature of the gospel?

The quotation from Habakkuk, rightly translated, throws light upon this difficulty; as it shows that the "righteousness of God"[1] in the first clause of the 16th verse cannot here mean God's own righteousness, *i.e.* righteousness in God Himself or in His own actings, but must mean the righteousness of a man who is put right with God by faith in God's righteousness. To understand the passage we must turn to the prophecy from which the quotation is taken, and to which the apostle evidently points as the key to his discourse.

Habakkuk had been commissioned to announce to his countrymen a terrible chastisement, in the form of a Chaldean invasion. He felt the grievousness of his country's sin and the righteousness of the divine indignation against it; but his knowledge of the true character of God soon enabled him, even in the full vision of the impending calamity, to take hold of the assurance that He would use punishment not for the destruction of the sinners but for their deliverance from the sin. "O Lord," he exclaims, "Thou hast ordained them

---

[1] The Scriptures afford other instances of this subjective form of expression, *e.g.* "Is there not yet any of the house of Saul, that I may shew the *kindness of God* unto him ?" (2 Sam. ix. 3.) "The *peace of God*, which passeth all understanding, shall keep your hearts " (Phil. iv. 7).

for judgment, and, O mighty God, Thou hast established them for correction." The prophet was *put right* with God by faith in this fatherly purpose; he looked forward to the blessed result, and that enabled him to accept with thankful submission the process, however painful, by which it was to be brought about.

He found the blessing of faith in its exercise; it was a deliverance, a redemption from fear and mistrust of God, and from the alienation consequent on such a state of mind. He was not rewarded for his faith in any other way than as a hungry man is rewarded for eating. His faith simply laid hold of God's purpose, and he was *justified* or made right with God by doing so. He thus possessed *the righteousness of faith.* Remark also that he made the first step towards it, before the vision of the final triumph of good was granted to him, by the simple exercise of his spiritual understanding. His own account of the way by which he arrived at peace is very instructive. He describes himself, when the announcement of the coming calamity is first made to him, as looking up to God and thus addressing Him— "Art Thou not from everlasting, O Lord my

God, my holy One?" And from the remembrance that God was *the holy One* he springs at once to this conclusion—"We shall not die."

It was after he had gained this sure standing-ground for himself and his own nation, that the further intimation was given to him that the ultimate result of all God's dealings with man would be the entire destruction of all evil. "The earth shall be full of the knowledge of the glory of the Lord, as the waters cover the sea." This blessed consummation might be long of coming, but he is encouraged to "wait for it" by the assurance that "though it tarry it will surely come, it will not tarry." The conviction that this was God's purpose enabled Habakkuk to welcome even the Chaldean invasion, and in the prospect of its near approach to sing that triumphant song with which his prophecy concludes, "Though the fig-tree shall not blossom, neither shall fruit be in the vines; the labour of the olive shall fail, and the fields shall yield no meat; the flock shall be cut off from the fold, and there shall be no herd in the stalls: yet I will rejoice in the Lord, I will joy in the God of my salvation."

The Apostle saw still more clearly than Habakkuk did, " that bow made quite naked" in heaven which, in spite of the present violence of the storm, gives the assurance of a coming blessing ; he also saw, under the wrath, an omnipotent righteous love which uses that wrath for its own purposes, and of which it is only the needful expression.

This gospel is indeed a blessed one, giving us the assurance that forgiveness in its deepest meaning is a permanent element in God's relation to us ; inasmuch as it declares that good shall ultimately triumph over evil, blessing over cursing, life over death. If we can adopt this hope and make it our own, if we can but see that God's holiness—His abhorrence, *i.e.* of all iniquity—is really a pledge that He will seek not to destroy us but it, in other words, to deliver us from it, we have our feet upon a rock, we have hold of a hope which cannot be taken from us. As soon as we distinctly see that it is more to the glory of God's holiness to turn us from sin than to punish us without reference to that as the object and result of the punishment, we are within sight of that peace which passeth all understanding ; for then the loudest thunders of conscience, instead of being prophetic of endless misery, become to us the sure witnesses of an untiring love which will never cease its efforts to separate us from all evil.

Faith in God as having this purpose is the spiritual condition which Habakkuk considers to be the only right condition for a man to be in; and the Apostle adopts the idea, and boasts of the gospel concerning Christ as " the power of God unto Salvation," " because therein," or perhaps better, " in him" (that is, in Christ the subject of the Gospel) is contained the revelation both of this righteous faith, and of that Divine love which is the full and sufficient foundation for all righteous faith or filial trust in man.

This then is the simple meaning of what has been called the Pauline doctrine of *justification by faith*, though other meanings have been given which have bewildered the minds of men and led them away from the simplicity of truth. But there can be no reason for calling it by his name, as all our Lord's personal teaching, and indeed all the teaching of the Old as well as of the New Testament, rests upon it.

It was even taught, as we have seen, implicitly by Socrates who had never heard of either, and who yet was, like Paul himself, a real apostle of the Gentiles though preceding him by some centuries. I believe that it is special neither to Judaism nor to Christianity, that it is in fact no peculiar doctrine, separable from others, but rather the intelligible sum and substance of all doctrine, and that the value of the special revelations of Christianity really consists in the illustration and corroboration which they give to it. For no one can doubt that faith or filial trust in God, as the Almighty Father who orders all events for the spiritual education and eternal good of His children, is the right condition of mind for spiritual beings, the condition which will best fit them for walking with God, and doing and accepting His will in the duties and events of life; in other words, that such faith is their righteousness.

Such an assurance as this I would call *true natural religion*, and I would even say that this naturalness is the test by which the truth of any revelation, claiming to be from God, must in the last resort be judged. I know that in speaking thus I run the risk of offending those who have been accustomed to think of natural religion as the mere product of man's own imagination and reasoning, and who therefore condemn it as the presumptuous rival and enemy of revealed religion; but I would explain that the religion which I call *natural* is not the production of man's reasoning or imagination, nor at all opposed to supernatural or revealed religion, but is itself a supernatural revelation to the heart of every individual testifying there to what is righteous, and proving itself, by the response of conscience, to be of God.

We are not therefore to imagine that when Paul preached the righteousness of faith, he thought he was announcing an altogether new principle, or that no such righteousness had been known till he preached it. He only assumed that whenever or wherever righteousness had appeared in man, its root was, and must have been, trust in a sovereign righteousness, because real righteousness always implies a sacrifice of self which nothing but trust can call forth. In his preaching of Christ crucified Paul showed the deepest ground of that principle, and thus gave it distinctness and prominence, but it was a principle on which, however dimly discerned, men must at all times have acted whenever they have in any measure attained to righteousness. The Eternal Son is the model of trust. In other words, self-sacrifice, which is necessarily implied in filial trust and obedience, is his eternal and essential characteristic, justifying the title given to him, "The Lamb slain before the foundation of the world." The sacrifice on Calvary was the manifestation in time of this eternal reality.

But can we really believe that Paul meant to represent the revelation of this righteous faith—this human righteousness (for though received out of God assuredly it is righteousness in man that is here spoken of) as that which made the gospel the power of God unto salvation? Is he not in so doing putting the effect for the cause? Is not the revelation of God's fatherly purpose the real cause—the real *power*—of which man's righteousness is only the result? It may be said doubtless that the revelation of a righteousness in man springing out of faith *implies* a character in God as the ground of such faith, without which the faith could not exist ; but, though this be so, we must still ask what reason the Apostle could have had for expressing himself in such an indirect and apparently illogical manner.

Two reasons may be suggested. In the first place, although the character and purpose of God were really occupying the Apostle's mind, yet the occurrence to him of the passage from Habakkuk might naturally have led him to express himself as he does, because that quotation directly refers not to the character of God which calls forth the faith of man but to the human character arising out of ($\dot{\epsilon}\kappa$) that faith. Moreover it is not an abstract principle but a living man that is there presented to us, "The man made right by faith shall live." It is natural for Paul to identify this "righteous man" with Jesus, and in his resurrection to see the literal fulfilment of the declaration " he shall live," that is, he shall overcome death ; especially as he had before said that Jesus was " declared to be the Son of God with power, *by the resurrection from the dead.*"

But there is another reason connected with the mode in which the Christian revelation was made which doubtless decided him to use this phraseology. That revelation was made *in the person of Jesus Christ.* It has been said that there is in the Eastern mind less demand for the accurate observance of distinction between the object and subject in religious thought than in ours; and it sometimes almost seems as if in Paul's hand the righteousness of faith becomes itself the gospel. This however is quite natural. Christ *is* himself both object and subject in Christianity. He both shows forth the Father's loving purpose which is the ground of all faith, and he lives by the faith which rests on that purpose. He is thus both the gospel itself, and in him is shown forth that righteousness by faith which is its most precious product. Thus whilst he is the *object* of faith as the Revealer of the Father, he is also the *exerciser* of faith as the Truster in the Father.

This seems to me not only to explain the Apostle's reason for choosing this way of expressing himself, but to confirm the suggestion that the words ($\dot{\epsilon}\nu$ $a\dot{v}\tau\hat{\omega}$) in ver. 17, rendered in the English version " therein," ought to be rendered " in him," *i.e.* in Christ. It may indeed be said that the gospel, not Christ, is the subject of the argument. St. Paul seems to be explaining how the gospel is "the power of God unto salvation," and this explanation, it may be contended, must consist in telling us what is contained *therein;* but let it be remembered that it is the gospel *concerning Christ*, and that assuredly all its virtue—all its "power"—must lie in what it tells us of *him*, that is, in what it reveals as existing "in him."[1]

This life-giving righteousness by faith is revealed in the history of Christ, and it is revealed for, or with a view to faith (εἰς πίστιν); that is, to bring all men under the influence of the same faith. Thus it is Christ's own faith that we are called to enter into—the faith of Habakkuk fully developed into the faith of the Son. Our faith *in* Christ—our belief, *i.e.* that he is the eternal Son, that he is our Head, and that as our Head he lived and died for us—is not in itself the faith *of* Christ, it is

---

[1] The three great and most ancient MSS. (S. V. and A.) omit τοῦ Χριστοῦ in ver. 16, but if we look back on the 3rd and 4th verses where the description is expanded, of what in the 16th verse is simply called the Gospel, we shall see that the latter is in fact merely an abbreviation of the former, and if we substitute the longer for the shorter statement, we shall find that the sense not only admits of the change but requires it.

only a belief concerning him which enables us to enter into and adopt *his* faith, the faith, *i.e.*, by which he himself lived.

I know that many will feel as if it were a lowering of Christ's position in relation to man to hold forth his faith in the Father as a model for us to follow, and that they will also feel it to be a misuse of terms to call this a gospel. They will say that it would be as reasonable to give such a name to the first commandment of the law as to give it to a call to follow the example of Christ. But if Jesus, being very man, tempted like as we are, subjected to all conditions of humanity, even to death, was enabled by the Eternal Spirit to offer himself in the self-sacrifice of filial confidence without spot of sin to his Father, there is certainly a great gospel in his being set forth to us *as an example*, because it contains the assurance that God is as truly our Father as He is his Father, and that consequently we have the same right to trust our Father and the same capacity of trust as he had. He could not otherwise be righteously set forth as an example at all. The proposal would become a cruel mockery.

Many may also shrink from this way of distinguishing between faith in the Father—that filial trust which was Christ's *own* faith—and belief in the Divine nature and work of Christ, and from looking on this last as only a stepping-stone to the former. It is however a distinction entirely recognised in the New Testament. Let me cite especially 1 Peter i. 18-21, where the Apostle says: " Ye were not redeemed with corruptible things . . . but with the precious blood of Christ . . . who verily was foreordained before the foundation of the world, but was manifest in these last times for you, who *by him do believe in God*, that raised him up from the dead, and gave him glory; *that your faith and hope might be in God.*" The fundamental and ultimate faith here spoken of is trust *in God ;* and the appearance of the Son in our nature and all that he did and suffered for us are discoveries to us of the deep grounds of that trust. In Jesus Christ—in his life, death, and resurrection—that righteousness of faith (of which Habakkuk speaks) is set forth in its true development of filial trust.

Faith in its deepest sense is not a belief in doctrines, although the belief of all true doctrines is helpful to our having faith. Whilst however I make this distinction between the faith which is the participation of Christ's own trust in the Father and that belief in himself—as the Son of God and Head of humanity—through which we may rise up into that ultimate faith, I also feel assured that St. Paul so apprehended the connection between faith in Christ and trust in the Father that he is not always careful to distinguish between them, conceiving that the one is involved in the other.

It will be observed that though there is no mention of forgiveness in this passage, yet the fullest forgiveness is implied in it. As sinners we cannot have filial trust in God, unless we believe that He forgives our sins; and as we are called to exercise this trust, we have in this call the assurance that He does forgive them. But forgiveness in its deepest sense does not mean deliverance from a penalty or the reversal of a sentence, it means the continuance of a fatherly purpose of final good, *even through the infliction of the penalty and the execution of the sentence.*

Jesus is set forth, suffering death as the penalty of sin in unswerving filial trust, as a manifestation to us of that righteousness which God desires to see in us. But surely this instructs us that under that same sentence of death, with all its precursors and concomitants, even when aggravated by the personal consciousness of sin, we are entitled and commanded to look to God as a loving Father who can make even these things work together for our progress in righteousness. In the truest theology forgiveness (taken in the sense of remission of penalty) is never considered as an ultimate blessing, but only as means to an end. *That end is righteousness.* It is always God's end in all His dealings with us, and He desires that it should be ours. He sent His Son, not to save us from punishment, but to save us from sin, to restore us to the paths of righteousness. This is His unchangeable purpose, and forgiveness, taken as an affirmation that it is so, is absolutely necessary as the foundation of all faith and consequently of all righteousness in man.

Christ did not come either to obtain the Father's forgiveness, or to justify Him in bestowing it. It was the Father's spontaneous forgiving love which sent him into the world to accomplish His purpose of educating man into righteousness. The language of Scripture is most decided on this point; it never represents Christ as reconciling God to man, but always as reconciling man to God.[1]

Chapter II.

The Jewish Scriptures from first to last had declared that it was not the purpose of God to restrict the knowledge of Himself to the Jewish family, but that from the beginning He had intended to bring the whole human race within the embrace of His love. In putting that family under His more immediate and palpable government He was setting up in them not only a type and witness of the unchangeable and permanent principles of His rule over all nations, but also a living channel by means of which these principles might be disseminated throughout the earth. It is worthy of remark that this large purpose of blessing for the whole race of man is repeated on every occasion when the special promise to Abraham

---

[1] See 2 Cor. v. 18-20 and Col. i. 20.

is given, so that it was really in contradiction to their most venerated oracles that the Jews were so slow to admit that the favour of God could rest on any who were not of their blood. " In thy seed shall all nations of the earth be blessed" is the unlimited announcement made to Abraham, which surely in its natural interpretation gives the expectation of eventual blessedness for every child of man, and which at least ought to have prepared the Jews to welcome all the other races to a share in their privileges. The rite of circumcision and the law of Moses distinguished and separated them from other nations. The promise of the seed united them to all. But they preferred distinction to union; they could not or they would not understand that they and those other nations stood on the same level before God; they did not see that true blessedness consists in righteousness, and that righteousness consists in the unselfish love of God and man, independent of caste or creed, of rite or ceremony.

Thus the question of Jewish superiority entered necessarily into the Apostle's discussion concerning the nature of righteousness and the way of attaining it. The Jew thought that there was a righteousness in being of the holy seed and in *possessing* a divinely constituted law.[1] Paul meets this thought by the self-evident proposition that righteousness cannot consist in having a law but in obeying it, and by maintaining that wherever the spiritual requirements of the law are complied with, there and there only righteousness is to be acknowledged, whether in Jew or Gentile. In his large thought he refused to limit righteousness to the profession of either Christianity or Judaism; he believed that amongst Gentiles as well as Jews there had always been individuals who "by patient continuance in well-doing had sought for glory, honour, and immortality," and that to all such God communicates eternal life. At the same time he believed that those well-doers must have become what they are by trust in a supreme good—a perfect righteousness—by trust in One who desires their

---

[1] This was not true Judaism, but the corruption into which Judaism had fallen. The true Jew trusted in the God of his fathers, because He was the only and righteous One who would therefore seek to make him holy and righteous. "I will direct my prayer unto thee, and will look up; *for* thou art not a God that hath pleasure in wickedness, neither shall evil dwell with thee."—Ps. v. 3, 4.

righteousness, and that such trust was most rare and exceptional, because almost universally men had formed for themselves a false conception of God, which made trust in Him as a righteous Father absolutely impossible.

"Therefore if the uncircumcision keep the righteousness of the law, shall not his uncircumcision be counted for circumcision? For he is not a Jew who is one outwardly, neither is that circumcision which is outward in the flesh; but he is a Jew who is one inwardly, and circumcision is that of the heart, in the spirit, and not in the letter, whose praise is not of men but of God."

The Apostle then supposes the Jew to reason thus,—"But surely our nation must have some advantage over others." "The real advantage," Paul replies, "consists not in any immunity saving the Jew from the necessity of righteousness, but in the access which his Jewish circumstances give him to those oracles of God of which his nation is the keeper, and in the help which he may derive from these oracles in his spiritual education." This advantage a carnal mind craving only ease and security could not appreciate. The Jew desired an imputed righteousness which cost him nothing, not considering that an imputed righteousness could only prove an imputed blessedness. He thought that the promises of God were made to Abraham and his seed according to the flesh, whereas they were really made to those who were not of the circumcision only, but who also walked in the steps of that faith of our father Abraham which he had yet being uncircumcised. The limitation of the blessing to the spiritual seed was not created by an arbitrary decree, but existed in the nature of things; righteousness and spiritual blessedness being one and the same thing.

What then? Are we (the Jews) better than the Gentiles? No, in no wise, for we have before proved both Jews and Gentiles, that they are all under sin. St. Paul follows this up by quotations from the Psalms, which declare in the strongest terms the universal corruption which prevailed. "As it is written, There is none righteous, no not one, there is none that understandeth, there is none that seeketh after God;" winding them up with this comment, "Now we know that whatsoever things the law saith, it saith to them who are under the law, that every mouth may be stopped, and all the world may become guilty before God. Therefore by the deeds of the law shall no flesh be justified in His sight, for by the law is the knowledge of sin." He certainly seems here to assume that the law itself, taken merely *as law* or commandment, does not contain an antidote to this evil state of things; it commands righteousness, but it does not disclose the principle or influence which may produce righteousness in the sinner.

Chapter III.

Much of the first and second chapters and a great part of the third are filled with terrible proofs of the evil consequences of departure from God through the want of faith both in Jews and Gentiles. The depravity was universal, not only amongst the ignorant but amongst the enlightened and cultivated, not only amongst the Gentiles, but amongst the Jews notwithstanding their superior light. The contemplation of this accumulated mass of iniquity seems to suggest the question, Is not something beyond this principle of trust now required? Trust may suffice to sustain a righteous man in righteousness, but how is it to deal with transgression? Can a man who is conscious of guilt, who feels himself lying under condemnation, trust in God as his Father? Is he entitled to do so? With this thought in his mind the Apostle seems led to the conclusion that, if filial trust is the only possible righteousness for a creature, there must be in the character of God Himself a foundation for such trust which no sin in man can overthrow; and he proceeds to show that ground for this assurance is contained in the revelation of Jesus Christ, " whom God set forth " as exercising that very trust even whilst suffering under the execution of the penalty which had been denounced against sin.

This is the advance made in the third chapter beyond the principle announced in the first. In that first statement human righteousness is declared to consist in filial trust, and when the question is moved, Can man under the condemnation of sin exercise this trust? it is answered by the appearance of Jesus actually exercising this trust whilst under this condemnation, and thus declaring that it was competent for every man to do the same.[1] From the beginning the trust was not to rest on any merit in the truster, but simply on the fatherly love of Him in whom the trust is placed, and seeing that filial trust is the root-principle through which alone true inward rightness of character as well as right actions can be produced, there was, according to the law of faith, no boasting before sin entered into the world any more than after. The Apostle therefore is not setting aside the law through faith, but establishing it.

In the 21st verse of the third chapter, St. Paul returns to the subject of the righteousness of faith, and to the manifestation of it in Christ Jesus. He is brought back to this subject by the conviction that it is a real substantial righteousness which is required, not a mere forgiveness of past sin; so that nothing con-

[1] It has been remarked that our Apostle is often in the habit of carrying forward his argument not so much by the way of premiss and inference as by the re-statement of the same idea with some addition or modification. He is following out this method most strikingly in these two passages.

ventional or ceremonial, even though instituted by God Himself, can supply what is wanting. Jew and Gentile stand on the same level, both being sinners and both requiring righteousness.

I am sure that many readers, imbued with the theology of later times, must have felt that up to this point there has been a defect in this Gospel of St. Paul. There has been no allusion in it to what they have been accustomed to consider the most important part of Christ's work upon earth, namely his vicarious sacrificial death as an atonement for the sins of the world, and they will now expect this defect to be filled up. I think that on candidly examining the passage they will find that the Apostle is only strengthening his former statement, and that the want which they feel is really filled up in that very statement, though not altogether in the way they expected. His words are " But now the righteousness of God without the law is manifested, being witnessed by the law and the prophets; even the righteousness of God which is by faith of Jesus Christ unto all and upon all them that believe; for there is no difference : for all have sinned and come short of the glory of God :

being justified freely by his grace, through the redemption that is in Christ Jesus ; whom God hath set forth *to be* a propitiation through faith in his blood, to declare His righteousness for the remission of sins that are past, through the forbearance of God ; to declare, I say, at this time His righteousness ; that He might be just and the justifier of him which believeth in Jesus."

I am aware that the doctrine of expiation through the vicarious death of Christ is sacred and precious to the hearts of many, nevertheless I am compelled to regard it as a human invention opposed to the true character of God. Christianity reveals God as a Father whose purpose is to train His children into a participation of the spirit and character of His Son. The "justification" therefore or vindication of His dealings towards us is not in the assurance that the claims of justice have been satisfied before He shows mercy, but in the discovery of this gracious purpose in those dealings, and in their fitness to accomplish it. Just as the righteousness of an earthly father consists in his purpose to make his children righteous, and cannot be conceived of as separate from it, and the vindication of his righteousness is the discovery of this purpose in all his conduct towards them.

The appearance of Jesus Christ on the earth was the expression of an infinite love already existing in the Father's heart. His coming into man's flesh whilst it lay under condemnation of death was the announcement that the sin of man had not changed God's fatherly purpose, and that, however overwhelming our sense of sin may be, we are yet called on—without any intervening process—*at once* (ἐν τῷ νῦν καιρῷ, *i.e.* in each successive present moment) to trust God as our Father, and thus to come into a righteous state. On this fact faith may always rest, and from it faith may always take a fresh start, into whatever sin we may have fallen.

It is a chief point in the teaching of Christianity that we should always have this assurance, and yet that it should be no encouragement to continue in sin. It reveals to us that according to the eternal necessity of things blessedness cannot be separated from that trust in God which constitutes righteousness, nor misery from that self-trust which constitutes sin; and that the very ground of our trust in Him is the unchangeableness of His purpose that we should be *righteous*. This unchangeableness is revealed in Christ, and we know that whatever our sin may have been, the favour of God always rests on him, and we as his members always participate—in a true and real sense—in that favour, and in order to be right with God have only to open our hearts to its influence. So long as we are not doing so we cannot but remain unrighteous and unblessed, but we must not allow ourselves to forget that this *is* our position; we must not, *i.e.*, interpret the condemnation of our own conscience as a declaration from God that He has cast us off, but rather as His declaration that, because He has *not* cast us off, He cannot permit us to go on separating ourselves from Him.

No suffering of a penalty due to sin either by ourselves or by another in our place can put sin away, for sin is a spiritual thing and can only be put away by return to righteousness; and, as sin has also a strictly individual character, it is only by becoming righteous ourselves, and not by another being so in our stead, that sin in us can be truly put away.

Salvation in its highest sense must be a personal and individual thing; and therefore in order to attain it each man must himself participate in the filial trust of Christ which is righteousness.

But although Christ's work is not substitutional or, in the ordinary sense of the word, vicarious, still it is work done *for* man in a sense applicable to the work of no other human being. He does nothing *instead of* us—nothing, that is, to save us from doing it; he does things *for* us that we also may in him have power to do them. He did not die to save us from dying, but that we might, in the power of an endless life, die with him, that we might by partaking in his death—by surrendering our life as he did into the hand of the Father in loving confidence—be also partakers of his resurrection. When he assumed our nature under all its evil conditions he *lived by faith*, he accepted sorrow and death in faith, it was the cup his Father had given him to drink, and in doing so he overcame death and him who had the power of death, thus by his example giving guidance and encouragement to every child of man. And further, he did this not as an individual but as the Head of the race; thereby lifting all humanity along with himself up from the bondage of corruption into the glorious liberty of the children of God. None certainly can enter into his victory except by partaking in his trust, but in that general elevation of the nature there must be contained real help for every man in his special work, as well as a pledge that He who has raised Jesus to His own right hand will not cease His labour of love till He has raised thither also the last and least of his members. In the victory of our Head He has given us an all-sufficient foundation for the most absolute trust, as well as a manifestation of the certain effects resulting from its exercise. None but a Son could have made this revelation, and none but those who are created in the Son could be capable of apprehending or receiving it. He came to draw and guide the hearts of the children back to the Father, and he did so by his own life of filial trust.

The faith spoken of in the 25th verse is I believe Christ's own trust in the Father—the trust which sustained him *even in the shedding out of his life-blood*. Faith, and the righteousness of faith, have been the theme of the epistle hitherto, and Jesus has been presented to us as the model of it, so that we ought to be prepared for what appears here to be the announcement that the propitiation consists in faith carried to its highest power, faith whilst shedding out the life-blood, that faith which says, "Father, into Thy hands I commend my spirit." I know that this interpretation is not commonly accepted, but the whole passage is generally acknowledged to be very obscure, and I shall endeavour to give some reasons in support of my conviction that it is the true one. I am well aware that the faith here spoken of is almost always assumed to be *our* faith, with as much confidence as the blood is assumed to be *Christ's* blood. But this is not the natural meaning. The preposition διά, necessarily by the construction connected with πίστεως, indicates faith as the process or instrument through which the propitiation was effected, or rather through which Jesus became a propitiation. But no one can suppose that *that* could be through *our* faith. Although the propitiation cannot profit us spiritually except through our believing it, yet surely it is not *our* faith which makes the propitiation; he himself made it, and by his own faith.

And if it was Christ's own faith it could not be "faith in his blood" in the ordinary acceptation of that phrase;[1] it must, as I have said, have been faith whilst he was shedding his blood. It was not his blood which made the propitiation, but his faith in shedding it —his perfect filial trust while suffering the accursed death of a criminal, the inherited penalty of sin to which by taking our nature he had subjected himself, and to the righteousness of which he, as Head of the race, set his seal by submitting to it.

His faith in death was the faithful summing up and completion of his life of faith. It was an act of entire self-sacrifice, the fullest and most perfect manifestation of the loving dependent recipiency by which the creature becomes partaker of the righteousness of God.

[1] " No such expression occurs in Scripture as faith in the blood, or even in the death, of Christ. Nor is πίστις followed by ἐν in the New Testament, though faith, like all other Christian states, is often spoken of as existing in Christ (Gal. iii. 26). The two clauses should therefore be separated, 'through faith'—'by his blood.'"—JOWETT'S *St. Paul's Epistles to the Thessalonians, Romans, Galatians*, vol. ii. p. 134, 2d edition (for part of note, see 1st ed. vol. ii. p. 121).

This was the propitiatory act; and God set forth His Son, in this act, as a manifestation of the righteousness which He desires to see in man. The righteous character of the act made it a propitiation; and as God desires to see righteousness in all men, He in fact desires to see that propitiation in all men.

It was not then Christ's blood which satisfied the Father's heart, but his faith whilst shedding it, his faith in laying down his life in fulfilment of the Father's will. This faith was the element of which the Apostle speaks as approved by God, as propitiating His spirit, and which he sets forth as the true manifestation of righteousness. This is the spiritual condition in which He desires to see us at all times, in each successive present moment (ἐν τῷ νῦν καιρῷ). But such an entire trust is only possible on the condition of there being a perfect love in God towards us which forgives even whilst it punishes all sin. We could not lie trustful in the hand of God if we thought that past sins were unforgivingly remembered against us. I would connect the clause διὰ τὴν πάρεσιν, κ.τ.λ. "on account of the passing over of foregone sins" with the clause "whom God set forth." God sent His Son into the world because foregone sins were passed over, and did not stand out as hindrances to His fatherly intercourse with men.

Thus then the faith of Jesus himself witnesses to the trustworthiness of the Father. He both manifests his Father's righteousness, and declares the righteousness of all who have the faith he himself had.

We are thus led on to the concluding clause of the 26th verse, "That he might be just, and the Justifier of him who believeth in Jesus." The meaning of this I believe is that because God is Himself righteous He is the communicator of righteousness to—or the Rightener of —him who had the faith which Jesus had. It is not justification in the forensic sense which is here spoken of. The Apostle's subject has all along been righteousness, not acquittal; if we forget this we lose the thread of the argument. The revelation is made "for obedience to the faith," that is, to bring men into submission to the will of God. But in this clause we leave the subjective and come to the objective; not indeed as a new thing, for all along we have seen that the subjective—the righteousness of

God in man—implies the objective, the righteousness of God in Himself. Still we welcome the change. It is God's own character which is the ground of all faith; and the setting forth of Jesus as the example of that faith is only gospel to us when understood as a discovery of the Father's purpose to make us partakers of His own righteousness.

By following out this train of thought I believe we shall arrive at the true sense in which Jesus is set forth as a propitiation. If we receive the idea that he is the organic Head of the race, and that everything which he did is in its principle to be reproduced in us; and if we further consider that, having subjected himself to all our conditions of weakness and suffering and death, he waged his successful war against our spiritual enemies simply in the might of filial trust, we can understand how the Father, looking upon him as he thus fulfilled all righteousness, should be well pleased. He saw in him the reflection of His own loving desire for the salvation of all men; He saw in him the completeness of that righteousness which He desires to see in them; He saw him also as their Head sending forth spiritual impulses through the whole body, inviting and enabling all the members to yield themselves to His Spirit;—He saw and was well pleased. He set him forth as the object of His entire complacency in that self-sacrifice which alone can put away sin. Once before the Father had borne witness by a voice from heaven, saying, "This is my beloved Son, in whom I am well pleased;" and the same witness is borne, not in word but in deed, when on the third day He raised him from the dead. In that word of witness "in whom I am well pleased" ($\dot{\epsilon}\nu\ \dot{\wp}\ \epsilon\dot{\upsilon}\delta\acute{o}\kappa\eta\sigma\alpha$) is to be found I believe the true meaning of "propitiation" ($\dot{\iota}\lambda\alpha\sigma\tau\acute{\eta}\rho\iota o\nu$) when understood as expressing the Divine judgment that Jesus was the fitting channel through whom the blessing of righteousness is to be communicated to the human race. In his Epistle to the Colossians the Apostle sums up the gospel which he was commissioned to preach in these words, "Christ in you the hope of glory," and as we meditate on them we may discover that they not only contain a full gospel to man but in some sense, with reverence be it spoken, a gospel to God also, the indwelling presence of the Son in every man being to the Father's heart the hope of glory for every man.

The righteousness of faith is revealed in Christ, the Head of our spiritual nature, for our belief (εἰς πίστιν), *i.e.* that we may actually possess it. Righteousness cannot be vicarious, yet its attainment may be facilitated by conditions which do not depend on our own actings but on those of another. We cannot be righteous or blessed without our own personal faith, but we are members of a body, the Head of which has essentially in himself the life of faith, and he is ever calling on us as members of his body to participate in it, assuring us that we have the same reason to trust in the Father as he himself has; and that though his life does not become ours until we partake in his faith, still its pulsations are felt in us when our conscience condemns our rejection of it, thus livingly witnessing that it is ours if we will only receive it. Jesus is presented to us as the true spiritual head of our race. He came into our flesh after it had fallen under the condemnation of death, and through his fulfilment of righteousness under these conditions, he has overcome death and nullified the condemnation. We are therefore no longer under a condemned Head, we are in the state which St. Paul describes in ch. v. 2 as a state of grace, standing under Christ. This does not refer to character but to condition ; we are put into Christ's standing that we may receive his spirit and his character. Thus is Christ's trust the pattern of man's righteousness, not slavishly to copy but livingly to reproduce by the indwelling of his Spirit.

According to this conception of the purpose of God in Jesus Christ, all those expressions which have been interpreted as if the forgiveness of sin had been purchased by the sacrifice accomplished on the cross, will be understood as teaching how the spiritual apprehension of the mind of God, manifested in that sacrifice, necessarily produces filial trust, and thus works participation in the character of the Son. The Apostle seems to indicate this as the natural result of the exposition given in this epistle of the meaning of Christ's work on earth, when after finishing his argument in chapter xi. he draws this conclusion in the opening of chapter xii.—" I beseech you therefore, brethren, by the mercies of God, *that ye present your bodies a living sacrifice;*" he refers apparently to this very passage, iii. 25, where he had spoken of Jesus as propitiating the Father by the sacrifice of himself, and urges that this sacrifice which—as Leader of the faith (ὁ ἀρχηγὸς τῆς πίστεως), *i.e.* Leader in the path of filial trust, the model and inspirer of trust—Christ had made, should be reproduced in them.

In virtue of our original constitution we are all indwelt by him, as the natural body, in virtue of the nervous system, is indwelt throughout by the brain; and his assumption of our flesh in its actual conditions qualifies him in a special manner to act for us, so that we may benefit by his actions and that they may in their spirit be reproduced in us. If we can really identify with Jesus of Nazareth that light within us which is ever calling us upward out of sin into righteousness, we shall feel that he is our true Head and Representative on whom the Father always looks with perfect complacency, seeing in him the fulfilment of that which He desires to see in each one of us. We shall feel that we have a property in him and in all his doings, he did them *for us*, he lived and suffered and died and rose on our behalf, as our Champion and Leader, he went through life and death to enable us to go through them also. Shall we not then regard his death as our own, and his grave as a refuge from the tyranny of the flesh and of all seen things, in which we may lay down our old man —all that is corrupt within us—and in his resurrection rise up new men cleansed from every taint, finding the fountain of our life henceforward not in ourselves but in him? "Ye are dead, and your life is hid with Christ in God."

"Where is boasting then?" the Apostle asks as the conclusion of the foregoing argument. "It is excluded." Evidently, if justification means righteousness, boasting is excluded, because the righteousness of filial trust is not a possession of our own, it is not self-originated but communicated to us, and also because it rests on the forgiveness of sin and consequently on an acknowledgment of unworthiness. Thus *all* boasting is excluded, national and sectarian no less than individual; for the righteousness of filial trust is equally accessible to all, and is independent of race or caste, and of all rites and ceremonies whatsoever. And yet the law is not made void but established; because by filial trust the spirit of man is brought to accept the whole will of God.

Chapter IV.

These ideas are further brought out in the following chapter, wherein Abraham's righteousness is shown to have consisted simply in trust—a trust which he had whilst yet in uncircumcision, and before the institution of any religious ordinances peculiar to Judaism. "What then shall we say of the righteousness of our father Abraham?" Shall we say that he found it according to the flesh, that is, by doing something to obtain it? For if so, he at least would have some ground for boasting. But this is not God's account of the matter; "for what saith the Scripture? Abraham trusted in God ($\dot{\epsilon}\pi\iota\sigma\tau\epsilon\upsilon\sigma\epsilon$ $\tau\hat{\wp}$ $\Theta\epsilon\hat{\wp}$), and that was counted to him for righteousness"—placed to his account as righteousness—reckoned, *i.e.*, by God, to be the right state for him to be in. The knowledge of the purpose of

God to bless him, and through him all the families of the earth, and the belief of His perfect trustworthiness, put Abraham in a right state in relation to God and to all things.

It is remarkable that in speaking of Abraham and his faith the Apostle makes no direct mention of the sacrifice of Isaac. We should have expected this to occupy a prominent place in the argument; but his object being to show that the promise was made, and faith in the promise accepted as righteousness, *before* the institution of circumcision—and that thus both the promise and the righteousness were unconnected with Judaism and as free to the Gentile as to the Jew—he satisfies himself with stating the first step in the patriarch's career of faith. Yet the history of Isaac's sacrifice is virtually referred to, for Abraham's faith in God as "the God who quickeneth the dead and calleth those things which be not as though they were" belongs to that history, and the promise, not *of* the Seed but *to* the Seed, that " in him all the families of the earth should be blessed," was also made in connection with it.[1]

Evidently the Apostle introduces the faith

[1] Compare Genesis xii. 2, 3, with xxii. 16-18.

of Abraham, as he had before introduced that of Habakkuk, to help the Jewish converts to apprehend the meaning of the faith of Christ, and to show them that he is setting forth no new principle, but one which had been recognised through the whole course of God's communications with their nation. Besides, the very mention of Abraham and of God's promises to him must have awakened the thought of that "Seed" in whom both Jews and Gentiles were to be blessed—that Messiah who was the special subject of the Gospel.

He may however have had another object in this reference to him. He may have intended thus to prepare the minds of the Jews in the church at Rome for what he was about to say of the relation in which Christ stood to the human race as a Head, and of the privileges which were to flow to them through that relation. The Jews always felt that their peculiar relation to God was connected with their descent from Abraham—that their national privileges were God's testimony to *his* faith. They could not indeed enjoy the spiritual blessings contained in the privileges without an actual participation in the faith, but the privileges themselves belonged to them simply in virtue of their descent. Abraham was thus not only by his example a preacher of the righteousness of faith, but was also, in acknowledgment of that faith, made a channel—in some sense a propitiation—through whom most important benefits were communicated to his descendants and to the whole world.

Let us follow the Apostle in his own way of bringing this out.

This faith of Abraham is set forth as that which really made him a righteous man; and then it is added " this was not written for Abraham's sake alone, that it was imputed to him; but for us also, to whom "—in like wise—" it shall be imputed if we believe " (or better, whilst we believe) " on Him who raised up Jesus our Lord from the dead ; who was delivered *for* (*i.e. because of*) our offences " *as a race*—he having assumed our nature, and having thus subjected himself to the death which our offences had drawn down on the nature—" and was raised again *for* (*i.e. because of*) our justification "— our rightening—*as a race*, far indeed from being yet accomplished in the members but anticipated in the purpose and foreknowledge of God, and actually accomplished in our Head. He has taken part with us in all our burdens and liabilities that he may deliver us from them; he has so bound himself to us that in his resurrection we have the pledge of our own life.

Let us pause over this passage, and ask ourselves whether we can accept the meaning which has been suggested. Jesus is said to have been delivered *for our offences*, evidently not *that we might offend, but because we had* offended; evidently also not for the offences of certain individuals but for the offences of the race; and then it is added, " he was raised again for our justification," which words, if we follow the same principle of interpretation, must mean—not that we might be justified but—on account of our justification, or, *because we are justified*. And not because certain individuals are justified, but because *we* —the race—are justified; whatever that phrase may mean. In other words, the resurrection of Christ is a result and proof of man's justification. We hesitate perhaps to adopt this interpretation, yet it is the natural one. The entire participation of Jesus in our lot and ours in his, his acceptance of all our evil circumstances that we might share in his victory over them, is unquestionably the point to which the Apostle would direct our attention, that by the example of Jesus we may be encouraged to follow in the "steps of that faith" which had burst the bands of death. He sets before us Christ the Conqueror of death, as the firstfruits of the whole humanity, the pledge of the ultimate resurrection and glory of the race, that we may be constrained to give ourselves up to God with the same entire and undoubted trust.

Chapter V.

The fifth chapter begins with a triumphant summing up of the blessings connected with, and rising out of faith—Being therefore justified or put into a right state of mind towards God by a belief of His loving purpose, we have peace with Him through our Lord Jesus Christ, through whom also we have access by faith into this grace or gracious position in which we stand (it being the very position in which he himself stands), and rejoice in hope of the glory of God. The appearance of the Eternal Son in our nature and his triumph over death as our Head occupy in the Apostle's mind the place which the vision of the future glory occupied in the mind of Habakkuk—and with greater substance and power, for in the resurrection of Christ he saw the commenced fulfilment of the prophecy of final victory. As he believed himself and all mankind to be included in Christ as their Head, he saw in *his* resurrection the pledge of their ultimate deliverance from sin and death, and meantime, in virtue of their relation to him, he saw them standing in the same environment of grace that ever surrounded him.

This I believe is the true meaning of the apostolical benediction with which St. Paul concludes his epistles. "The grace of our Lord Jesus Christ be with you all," not the grace bestowed by Christ but the grace in which Christ himself stands, and of which the Apostle elsewhere specifies the composing elements,— "the love of God and the fellowship of the Holy Spirit." By this interpretation we escape that infringement of the hierarchical order in the latter passage involved in placing the name of the Son before that of the Father, which otherwise must be accepted.

The Apostle, consciously standing in this grace and speaking in the name of all who were partakers in the same faith, says, "We rejoice in hope of the glory of God," in hope, *i.e.*, of the fulfilment of Habakkuk's vision: "The earth shall be filled with the glory of God, as the waters cover the sea." And this expectation enables him to rejoice also in the process needed for its accomplishment. He looks forward to the great result, and understands the connection between that result and all the steps of the process. He glories in tribulations because he sees that they work patience, and that patience works experience of God's supporting hand, and that experience of past support works hope for the future—a hope that is not disappointed, "because the love of God is shed abroad in our hearts by the Holy Spirit which is given to us."

"For when we were yet without strength, in due time Christ died for the ungodly. For scarcely for a righteous man will one die, yet peradventure for a good man some would even dare to die; but God commendeth His love towards us, in that while we were yet sinners"—while yet under the righteous sentence of death—" Christ died for us."

It is worthy of remark that in this passage Christ's death is mentioned simply as a measure of God's love, no reason being given why His love should have taken this form. Does not this suggest that the words which follow, "being justified *by*" (or rather *in*) " his blood," may be interpreted in the subjective sense? being " set right " with God by our belief in so great a love, a love which could make such a sacrifice? for it is not the shedding of Christ's blood which sets us right with God, but our trust in the love which shed it. Whilst we were yet sinners—consciously deserving of rejection—God commended His love towards us, in that Christ died for us; saying while he did so, " He that hath seen me hath seen the Father." It is not expiation that is here spoken of, but a manifestation of love towards sinners on the part of a righteous God, who knows that the only way by which they can be brought back into righteousness is by trust in love.

Yet surely we cannot separate the form

which God's love took—the blood-shedding of His Son—from the relation in which Christ stands to us as our Head. Love took this form, because it was the form needed for the accomplishment of its object. He was delivered on account of our offences, he died as the Head of a race which had incurred the penalty of death, he accepted in filial trust their sentence, and thus acknowledged its righteousness; accepting it not merely as a penalty but as part of the process by which men were to be restored to righteousness. Thus Christ delivered men from the terrors of death by accompanying them into it; winding up by anticipation this stage of human existence, and by the outpouring of his Spirit giving to the race a new spiritual commencement of which each individual may avail himself. Yet it is not the payment of a debt, either for us or by us, which is to be the ground of our confidence, but that love of God which through the life and death and resurrection of His Son seeks our righteousness. God commendeth His own love towards us, in that, *while we were yet sinners*, Christ died for us.

The Apostle continues—Much more then,

being justified, that is, set right, by this manifestation of love in his death, we shall be saved (through our knowledge of his relation to us) from all apprehension of wrath. For if when we were enemies to God—opposed to Him through self-seeking and distrust—we were reconciled to Him by the manifestation of His love in the death of His Son, much more, being reconciled, we shall be saved by the knowledge and power of his risen life as our Head, seeing that we are called and destined to participate in that life. "And not only so, but we also joy in God, through our Lord Jesus Christ, through whom we have now received the reconciliation" (marginal reading)—" Wherefore as by one man sin entered into the world, and death by sin; and so death passed upon all men, for that all have sinned, for until the law"— or previous to the law—" sin was in the world, but sin is not imputed where there is no law"— sin therefore must have been inherited from a head—" nevertheless death reigned from Adam to Moses, even over those who had not sinned after the similitude of Adam's transgression, who is the figure of him that was to come."

These three last verses on the headship of

Adam are evidently intended by the Apostle as an introduction to what he has to say of the headship of Christ and of the relation in which Christ stands to the human race. He assumes that Adam's sin had brought death upon all his descendants, even upon those who had not sinned after the similitude of his transgression, that is, although they had not personally incurred the sentence; and the 13th verse seems to be inserted simply with the view of confirming this idea. Sin and death had been inherited by the whole human race, even by those who had not personally sinned, who therefore had not *earned* death, but were under sin and death in consequence of their descent from Adam. We are thus, each one of us, born with a proneness to sin and under sentence of death. What are we to think of such a constitution? What are we to think of Him who is its author?

In his deepest heart St. Paul always assumes the righteousness of God as the foundation of all things, and therefore when he sees anything in the ordering of the world which has the appearance of unrighteousness, he is prepared to expect some great counterbalancing manifestation which shall justify God by showing a result of good abounding out of it and over it. His argument in the present case is to this effect. Man, as being both carnal (σαρκικός) and spiritual (πνευματικός), has two Heads corresponding to these two natures— Adam and Christ—who by their respective characters and actions essentially affect the whole condition of the race and of all the individuals composing it, independently of any doings or deservings of their own.

In the actual condition of the world, lying in sin and subject to sorrow and death, we see the consequence of our relation to Adam. The Apostle has no desire and makes no attempt to soften the horror of the spectacle, but he turns directly from it, and reasons thus : If God has permitted such evil to come to us from the one head, He must have the intention that a counterbalancing good should come to us from the other—a good which may in all respects meet and overcome the evil. "For if by one man's offence death reigned by one, *much more* they which receive abundance of grace and of the gift of righteousness shall reign in life by one, Jesus Christ." As the evil is universal, not passing over a single individual, so must the good be; and as it is not outward evil only—a sentence of physical death resting on all—but a spirit of moral corruption working within all, so must it be as to the good.

The meaning of the 15th verse is somewhat obscure in the English version. St. Paul evidently means to state a parallelism between the offence and the free gift; that is, between Adam and Christ, yet the words seem to deny it. All thoughtful readers must feel this difficulty, but it is generally explained by supposing that the Apostle saw such abounding grace coming through Christ beyond the evil derived from Adam that his mind was more occupied with the difference than the resemblance. I am satisfied that instead of denying the paralleleism of the offence and the free gift he meant most emphatically to affirm it; and this he does very naturally by a negative interrogation. But as the offence, is not the free gift also? or rather, Ought it not to be so also? For if through the offence of the one head—Adam—the many be dead, that is, all except the one —as in a monarchy we say the one rules the many—much more it may be assumed, from the character of God, that His grace and the gift by grace, which is by the other Head— the one man Christ Jesus—hath abounded also unto the many, that is, to all.[1]

The grammatical construction of the 16th verse indicates, that instead of δι' ἑνὸς ἁμαρτήσαντος, "through, or by, one that had sinned," we should read δι' ἑνὸς ἁμαρτήματος, "through, or by, one sin," because the *one*, in the two former clauses of the verse, seems to be contrasted with the *many offences* (πολλῶν παραπτωμάτων) in the last clause; and also because throughout the passage wherever the numeral εἶς (*one*) occurs indicating a person—*i.e.* one of

---

[1] This argument of cumulative inference, expressed in the phrase, *much more* and *how much more*, appears frequently in the Bible. Thus, "If God so clothe the grass of the field which to-day is and to-morrow is cast into the oven, shall He not *much more* clothe you, O ye of little faith?" Can we suppose that God will care for the lesser and neglect the greater! If His love of order and beauty shows itself so wonderfully in the material creation, in the movements of the heavenly bodies, in the forms and colours of flowers, are we not sure that in the world of spirit His love will never rest until there also it has accomplished its perfect work? Again, "If ye, being evil, know how to give good gifts unto your children, how *much more* shall your heavenly Father give the Holy Spirit to them that ask Him?" The very existence of a good earthly father is to the spiritual reason a demonstration of the universal and surpassing fatherhood of God; the best earthly father being but an emanation from Him, a faint image of His fatherliness.

the two personal Heads—it is invariably accompanied by the article (τοῦ), which is not the case here. "And, as the judgment came by one sin or offence, is not the free gift parallel to it? for the judgment—after that one offence—became universal condemnation, but the free gift became—after many offences—through an opposite act of righteousness, universal justification; that is, it brought all men (notwithstanding the multitude of past sins) under a purpose of grace." "For if by one offence death reigned through the one head, much more"—we may infer from the goodness of God—"they who accept the abundance of grace and of the gift of righteousness shall reign in life through the other, Jesus Christ."

In the 18th verse we have manifestly the subjective idea of righteousness presented to us—the righteousness of faith—to counteract the tendencies of our descent from Adam. "The abundance of grace" can be received only through faith, the recipient organ. "Therefore, as, by the offence of the one, judgment came on all men to condemnation, even so, by the righteousness of the other, the free gift came upon all men unto justification of life" (εἰς δικαίωσιν ζωῆς), (the same word which is used in the last verse of the preceding chapter) as the moving-spring of that process by which all men shall ultimately be brought into living righteousness. "For as by one man's disobedience the many were made sinners, so by the obedience of the other shall the many be made righteous."

The whole passage is one of special pregnancy. In the first place, establishing, as a fundamental principle of St. Paul's theology, the ultimate salvation of the whole human race, and in the second, showing how the idea of Headship really explains and fulfils all that is supposed to be contained in the doctrine of substitution, even in the estimation of those who hold it most strongly. The difference lies in this, that according to the idea of Headship Christ acts organically *for* (ὑπέρ) men, in order that by what he does his spirit may be reproduced in them, while according to the doctrine of substitution he acts *instead of* (ἀντί) them, and to exempt them from acting.

"Moreover, the law entered (*i.e.* came in by the way or by parenthesis) that the offence might abound." I believe that the "law" is here the principle of law, including the law of Moses and all institutions which address and awaken the conscience. It entered or manifested itself, "that the offence might abound," that is, be largely felt in the consciences of individuals, convincing them that it was not merely for an hereditary taint or an offence of their forefather that they were suffering, but that they themselves were personally guilty. But where sin thus abounded grace still abounded over it, that as sin had reigned in the infliction of death, even so might grace reign through righteousness unto eternal life.

Chapter VI.

I am sure that every one who has attentively followed the Apostle through his argument will admit that he has not really laid himself open to a charge of antinomianism. And yet the charge must have been made, or he would not have felt it necessary to reply to it. Perhaps the prominent place given to the forgiveness of sin in all Christian teaching may have led to such an accusation, especially when connected with the universal practice in the early Churches, of recognising all who were admitted into their communion, however polluted their former lives may have been, as pure and holy. With this charge he deals in the following verses.

"What shall we say then? Shall we continue in sin, that grace may abound? God forbid! How shall we who are dead to sin live any longer therein? Do you not know that so many of us as were baptized into Christ Jesus were baptized into his death; so that we are buried with him, by this baptism into his death?" As the death of Christ was the embodiment of self-sacrifice, so our spiritual participation in his death would be truly a death unto sin, and as our baptism is a profession of such participation the Apostle would be justified in meeting the suggestion "shall we continue in sin that grace may abound?" by asking, "How shall we, who are dead to sin, live any longer therein?" He would I believe have been justified in thus meeting it; yet I would suggest that the Greek ($\tau\hat{\eta}$ $\dot{a}\mu a\rho\tau i\dot{a}$) both here and in verse 10 may be rendered *by* sin. How shall we who are dead *by* sin live any longer therein? If this be St. Paul's meaning then his answer is just an appeal to the common sense of men, implying a charge of absurdity and self-contradiction on the objectors. If we have already become subject to death, and have even died by sin, and have thus experienced that its natural effect is death, how is it possible that we should either expect or find life in it? In fact the objection is a very unfair one—for the Apostle through the whole course of his discussion has been inquiring, not how grace or forgiveness of sin may be obtained, but how righteousness itself can be arrived at, and he introduces grace in the concluding verse of the 5th chapter, as reigning "through *righteousness* unto eternal life." By bringing forward this objection he however shows that it was one which, although unreasonable, was yet frequently made, and which required to be specially dealt with. And accordingly he proceeds to show how the whole Christian doctrine is essentially antagonistic to sin itself. He had begun by laying down the principle that righteousness is the product of trust, and then he shows how full our warrant is for holding such a trust. We might then have expected that he would have maintained his position by simply insisting that trust in God, being itself man's right state, cannot possibly produce sin, and therefore that the declaration of the grace of God which alone can call forth that trust is the only true preaching of righteousness. At all events we had reason to expect that the argument by which he defended his doctrine would have been connected with the statement which he gives of it in the opening of the Epistle. And as we naturally desire to find logical coherence in a discourse, we should have welcomed the reappearance here of the principle of faith, as the power of God unto salvation.

But though there is a change in the form, there is a perfect continuity in the sense. We saw, in the 17th verse of the first chapter, that the revelation of the righteousness of faith was given to us in the person of Jesus Christ, who was set before us as the *model truster;* so that in fact we are called upon to be trusters when we are called upon to abide in him, and the original line of reasoning is continued when the Apostle, after having in the 5th chapter presented him to us as our spiritual head and fountain of righteousness, proceeds here to urge upon us the consequences of this relationship and the obligations arising out of it. For thus we are assured of our right to partake in his trust, and are invited to pass with him through all the steps of his progress to the upper glory. Our baptism into him is, according to the Apostle, specially a baptism into his death, a recognition that we were personally included in it, and are called to partake in its spirit. Therefore we were virtually buried with him by this baptism into his death —and to this end, that " like as Christ was raised from the dead by the glory of the Father, we also should walk in newness of life. For if we have been united with him in the likeness of his death, we shall be also in the likeness of his resurrection ; knowing this, that our old man is crucified with him, in order that the body of sin in us (the flesh, that part of our nature which yielded to the power of sin) might be destroyed or paralysed, that thenceforth we should not serve sin ; even as *he* by dying has been set free from all temptations to, and all claims of sin."

I do not think that St. Paul means here to state it as a general principle, that by death a man is set free from sin and its consequences; I rather think that as Christ's Headship is at present his theme, so it is Christ's own death in its speciality which he here presents to us, as that in which we are, in virtue of our relationship to him, actually involved, and in which we are called to participate spiritually and consciously.

"Now if we be dead with Christ we believe that we shall also live with him, knowing that Christ, being raised from the dead, dieth no more; death hath no more diminion over him; for in that he died he died *by* sin" (that is, under the penalty of sin, and as it were by the hand of sin) " once, but in that he liveth he liveth *by* God," that is, by the life and love and power of God.

Observe here how the Apostle hastens to show that his object is to inspire us with the confidence that, in virtue of our relation to Christ, his sufferings and their glorious result are ours. Even so reckon yourselves (through your relationship to him) to have verily shared in his death by sin, and now seek to share in that resurrection-life to which he has been raised. Take his resurrection as a pledge of your final triumph, and be bold to resist all attempts of sin to reign over you. Yield not to its usurpation—for it is a usurpation, it has no right to rule over you—but yield yourselves to God as those who have been raised from the dead, and your members as instruments of righteousness unto God. And be encouraged in this conflict by the assurance that sin shall not have dominion or finally prevail over you, for "ye are not under the law but under grace." If ye were under the law, sin *would* have dominion over you, for as there is no forgiveness according to the law, sin's claim upon you could never be got over, but ye are under grace—under a continual purpose of God that you should become righteous, which purpose contains a permanent forgiveness, and is a continual ground of filial trust. Ye are so included in Christ's death that ye may at every moment lie down in his grave as your own, and leaving there all bygone sins, recommence life afresh as free men unburdened by past guilt.

"What then? Shall we sin, because we are not under law but under grace?" The Apostle seems to have felt as if it were foolish to use the forms of reasoning in so plain a matter—he seems to say, "Cannot you use your common sense?" Is it not evident that to whom you yield yourselves servants to obey, his servants ye are to whom you so yield yourselves,—and that you must accept the wages of the master whose service you thus choose? The object of grace is not to change the nature of sin or of its service or of its wages, but to induce you to choose another master. The evil of sin does not consist in its producing misery or death, but in its essential contradiction to rightness."

In writing to the Corinthians[1] the Apostle speaks not of death as being the sting of sin but of sin as being the sting of death, and, throughout the epistle with which we are now engaged, his object has been to inquire not how grace or forgiveness may be obtained, but how righteousness may be acquired, and when he introduces grace it is that he may show how, when truly received, it produces righteousness. His strong feeling on this matter is very remarkably expressed in the verse which I have now paraphrased, "Know

[1] 1 Cor. xv. 55, 56.

ye not that to whom ye yield yourselves servants to obey, his servants ye are to whom ye obey; whether of sin unto death or of obedience unto righteousness?" We might have expected that as he had said "of sin unto death," he would have completed his parallel by saying "of righteousness unto life;" but when he thought of righteousness it doubtless appeared to him to be itself the ultimate good, desirable not for its best consequences but for its own intrinsic preciousness.

Chapter VII.

The 7th chapter is occupied with the subject of law, and its influences on the character. Although the Jewish law is referred to by the Apostle in the beginning of the chapter, it is only as an illustration of the argument, for the principle of law in the conscience, as contrasted with grace, is his real theme throughout. This is evident from the 5th verse. "For when we were in the flesh, the motions of sins which were by the law did work in our members to bring forth fruit unto death." His great subject, as we know, is righteousness—the righteousness which is founded on a true apprehension of the relation in which we stand to God as our forgiving Father; and he desires to guard against the misinterpretation of the principle of law, because, if misunderstood, although it seems to commend itself to the conscience it really bewilders it. If the law is not seen to be in harmony with the forgiving mercy of God and His fatherly purpose to deliver us from sin—if it discovers to us that we have incurred His condemnation without showing us any way of deliverance—its tendency must be to awaken in us a sense of guilt, and consequently to alienate us from God. It is to law, thus misunderstood, that Paul says " we are dead through the body of Christ " (that is, through our partaking in his death and in the faith which sustained him under death), " that we should be married to another, even to him who has been raised from the dead, that we should bring forth fruit unto God." Christ is the true law, being the personification of the righteous will of God which is ever seeking to reproduce itself in the hearts of all men, and actually accomplishing its object in so far as the love which gave Christ is apprehended.

But it is no misunderstanding of the law to suppose that it condemns sin and pronounces the penalty of death upon sin. The death of Christ was his acknowledgment, as Head of the race, that the sentence was righteous. The misunderstanding consists in not apprehending that it was our Father's love which gave the law and ratified the sentence, and that the sentence itself is remedial, being part of the process by which He would train us into His own likeness. Grace does not lower the demands of the law, or abrogate, or even soften down, its sentence. Rightly understood, law is the delineation of the righteousness and blessedness for which God created us, and its sentence of sorrow and death on disobedience is just the outward expression of that eternal self-executing principle which proportions the true spiritual life and enjoyment of the creature to the measure in which it has attained to, or fallen short of, that righteousness.

We are created *for* righteousness, not *in* it, that being impossible; but we are created in Christ Jesus, and are therefore capable of entering into his spirit, of understanding the

Father's loving purpose towards us, and thus of receiving the sorrow and death awarded by the law as a part of that education by which He would accomplish His purpose. The full understanding that God's condemnation of sin is not for destruction but for correction is necessary to the full understanding of the law. The co-existence of that condemnation with an inexhaustible purpose to make us partakers of His own blessedness, is the great revelation of Christianity.

In the latter part of the 7th chapter the Apostle describes the conflict which takes place within a man whose conscience is fully awake to the excellency of righteousness and to the unchangeable obligation of the law which requires it, whilst yet ignorant of the full grace of God. He makes his exposition peculiarly striking by speaking in the first person, thus giving the impression that it is the history of his own personal experience which he is disclosing. He sets before us three different stages of the spiritual life—the first characterised by unconsciousness of any moral demand upon us, corresponding to natural childhood though not necessarily limited to that period, as indeed with perhaps the majority of mankind it fills the whole earthly existence. "I was alive," he says, "without the law once, I had no sense of being under condemnation, but when the commandment came home to me the sense of sin like a serpent that had been asleep rose up within me and I died,—I felt myself under its condemnation, and thus the commandment, which seemed intended to point out the path of life, I found to be unto death." "Was then that which is good made death unto me? God forbid, but sin, that it might appear sin, working death in me by that which is good; that sin by the commandment might appear exceeding sinful." "Had I remained unconscious of the evil in me I could never have known what righteousness means, nor have learned to comprehend and appreciate the contradiction which exists between what I am and what I was intended to be. Had I not learned the evil of my selfish desires and my own inability to subdue them I could never have felt my need of God, of His forgiving love, and of His quickening, helping Spirit. This good then the law has done to me. It has discovered to me the truth concerning myself, it has discovered to me that I am in a wrong condition, and that while I remain in it I must be miserable." This is the Apostle's second stage, preparing the way for the joyful deliverance which is the last stage.

"For we know that the law is spiritual, but I am carnal, sold under sin. For what I do, I know not; for what I would, that do I not; but what I hate, that do I. Now if I do that I would not, it is no more I that do it, but sin that dwelleth in me." He thus finds that he has two selves—a sinful and a righteous self,—or rather perhaps that sin and righteousness are both parts of his being, and that he himself stands between them; and not at all, in this individual instance, as an indifferent looker-on, for he delights in the law of God after the inward man, and yet he is forcibly carried in the opposite direction by the law of sin in his members. He seems thus doomed to a hopeless internal strife, in which his efforts after good are always destined to be overborne. Under this oppressive consciousness he cries out, "O wretched man that I am, who shall deliver me from the body of this death—from the power of this flesh within me, which is keeping me in a state of sin, and is forcing upon me continually the wages of sin?"

And here St. Paul, who had begun his high argument by the glorious declaration, "I am not ashamed of the gospel of Christ, for it is the power of God unto salvation," answers the cry by bearing renewed testimony to the sufficiency of that salvation, and by repeating the same boast as an accomplished reality, "Thanks be to God, there is deliverance, and it is to be found in Jesus Christ our Lord; I have found it." This note of triumph is then followed up with a clause which in its form appears to be the resumption of the whole preceding passage, "So then with the mind" or conscience "I myself serve the law of God, but with the flesh the law of sin." In form, I say, this is a resumption of what is gone before, nevertheless it disappoints us by seeming to leave the conflict in its original state. It is obvious from the whole context that the writer means no such thing, for nothing can be more confident than his language in the second and third verses of the 8th chapter.

Yet, in several of those which follow, his prevailing tone is that of earnest warning, the note of triumph has passed away, and he speaks to his disciples like one who sees a great danger threatening against which he would guard them. Evidently this is the thought which gives its singular character to that concluding clause of the 7th chapter, which is just the text on which the exhortations of the 8th are founded.[1] In that clause he most distinctly teaches that the deliverance through Jesus Christ, for which he had given thanks, had not put an end to the conflict. It had put an end to its hopelessness, but the flesh still remained as an element of man's being, and still continued to be enmity to God, and St. Paul felt and testified concerning himself that the

[1] It cannot be denied that the clause comes in abruptly, and almost gives the impression that the Apostle meant to qualify the note of triumph which preceded it. The language of Scripture is addressed to the heart and conscience, not to the logical faculty, and, to be rightly understood, must be interpreted not in the letter, but in the spirit; that is, it must be interpreted in consistency with the two principles—(1) that it is the purpose of God to educate all men into righteousness; and (2) that human righteousness consists in man's will receiving and adopting the will of God. Unless it be so interpreted, its warnings and threatenings will naturally produce either a fear destructive of confidence in God and His revelations of grace, or an indolent security, or perhaps in some minds the one may simply neutralise the other.

moment he ceased to keep it under the control of the Spirit, that moment he fell into the service of sin. Grace operates not by annihilating the flesh or by making it better, but by enabling us to have our habitual thoughts and desires and interests, not in the flesh, but in the love of God and in fellowship with Him.

Chapter VIII.

Thus grace does not dispense with our exertions, but encourages us to make them by the assurance of success. The way of success which it points out is to be spiritually-minded, that is, to set our affections on things above, not on things on the earth; and the fundamental blessing of the gospel is that it enables us to be spiritually-minded by the revelation which it makes of the treasures which we have in heaven, and by its urgent call on us to *make* them our treasures, to know them as our eternal life and joy, and *so* to live in them that we may be out of the reach of the flesh.[1] Any

---

[1] Faith does not change the nature either of the good or of the evil principle within us. It operates not by making the

direct efforts against evil must be comparatively ineffectual. When passion or appetite, covetousness or vanity, presents a gratification which my sentient nature recognises as a reality, my surest defence lies in my living in a higher atmosphere and amongst joys which commend themselves to me as *more* real, because they address a higher part of my being. The gospel becomes to us the *power* of God unto salvation by introducing us into this higher atmosphere, and by making us acquainted with these better joys; and we are throwing away the help which it offers when, instead of endeavouring to live in that atmosphere and to familiarise ourselves with these joys, we content ourselves with only protesting against evil when it makes its assaults. Undoubtedly that was the state of the man whose unsuccessful and

---

flesh good but by helping a man to live "in the spirit;" that is, in that part of his being which is in contact with and can receive the Spirit of God. This agrees with our Lord's teaching (Matt. xii. 35), "The good man, out of the good treasure of his heart, bringeth forth that which is good: and the evil man, out of the evil treasure, bringeth forth that which is evil," intimating that the goodness of the good man does not consist in his having no evil treasure, no flesh ($\sigma\acute{\alpha}\rho\xi$) in him, but in his refusing to make it his treasure—to bring it forth or to live in it; and that the evil of the evil man, in like manner, does not consist in his having an evil treasure, but in his making it his treasure—bringing it forth, living in it.

wretched though honest conflict is described in chapter vii., and, if it was the Apostle's own conflict which he there describes, it was assuredly his consciousness that this was indeed its character which made him subjoin to his thanksgiving for deliverance that solemn note of warning which is contained in the clause we have been considering.

Let me here draw the reader's attention to a remarkable change which has been taking place in the language of the Apostle, in his treatment of his great argument. When he began, his whole mind seemed occupied with the idea of faith; the word occurs continually, but now, from the 2d verse of the 5th chapter, he has never named it, and never does again till the 30th verse of the 9th chapter. How are we to explain this? Has he really changed his ground, or has he only varied his expression? and what reason had he for this variation?

Perhaps the true explanation is that he made it unconsciously, led simply by the natural course of his exposition. And it is not difficult to understand and trace that leading. We must bear in mind that his subject is not faith but justification by faith, and consequently that his purpose is not to insist dogmatically on the necessity of *faith*, but to explain how faith produces *righteousness*. In fact the nature of righteousness is his real subject, and faith is treated of only in relation to it. He says that righteousness consists in the development of faith in God, and he makes the value and efficacy of the gospel to lie in the revelation of this faith given in the person of Jesus Christ, who was himself the eternal Truster, and in whom we were created that we might participate in his trust. Thus "abiding in him" comes to be the truest expression of faith in its full development. Then again, though our creation in Christ confers on us the capacity of entering into his faith, it does not *save* us—that is, it does not produce righteousness—unless the capacity be exercised. It is this consideration I believe which leads the Apostle to the adoption of the phraseology of the 8th chapter, in which spiritual-mindedness occupies the same place that faith does in the early chapters.

Possibly Paul may have intended, by varying his expression, to save the Roman disciples from a conventional and technical use of the word faith, perhaps also to conform his own teaching to that of the other apostles. That incorrect reports of his teaching had been brought to Jerusalem appears probable, and certainly St. James had felt that this doctrine of faith was liable to be misunderstood and perverted. It is remarkable that the meaning which he attaches to the word is quite different from that in which St. Paul uses it, and approaches very nearly to the idea of a *creed*, or formula of faith. It is only thus that we can understand how he should (in opposition to what we should conceive the natural idea of them) describe faith as the *body*, and works as the *spirit*. He is thinking of faith as a belief of facts, and of works not merely as things done (ἔργα), but as the living principle (ἐνέργεια) which produces them. With St. Paul on the other hand faith means the spirit of filial trust, implying that God is essentially and necessarily the Father of every man, and thus the proper object of trust for every man, and works mean not actions produced by such a trust, but all efforts to obtain a ground of confidence in ourselves, even by the observance of institutions appointed by God Himself. It is conceivable that St. Paul knew suspicions of his teaching to be entertained by some of the Christian teachers, and that he wished to remove these suspicions by language which he was sure they would acknowledge and respond to. And certainly the language of chapter viii. is of this kind.

It has been said that our Lord's discourses, and the sermon on the mount especially, teach justification not by faith but by works. Surely this is a great mistake, for is not the whole of that teaching based on the fact that God is truly and unchangeably our Father, and that even whilst we are feeding on husks with the swine, He is calling on us to return to Him as His children? And this I believe is precisely that doctrine of justification by faith which St. Paul insists on with such earnestness. It may be admitted that he is often abrupt, and that the occurrence of a particular word sometimes makes him start off on what appears to be a different train of thought, but no one can doubt that there is a real and substantial consistency in his treatment of his subject. We may however in a manner admit this consistency and yet not really perceive it. For instance, some who would never dream of questioning his inspiration might yet find a difficulty in discerning the oneness of his adopted text from Habakkuk, "The just by faith shall live," with his own words in chapter vi., "If we be dead with Christ we believe that we shall also live with him," or with those in the chapter we are now considering, "If ye live after the flesh ye shall die, but if ye through the Spirit do mortify the deeds of the body, ye shall live." Evidently unless faith, dying with Christ, and spiritual-mindedness mean the selfsame thing, he is pointing out three different ways of arriving at eternal life; but this is inconceivable. Faith, dying with Christ, and spiritual mindedness must therefore with St. Paul imply one another.

But to proceed; after giving the solemn warning in the close of the seventh chapter, the Apostle returns to the note of triumph which precedes that warning, with the purpose of explaining in what the deliverance through Jesus Christ consists. To understand his explanation, we must remember that the wretched condition out of which the complainer had cried for deliverance was an incapacity to resist the evil which he condemned, and to do the good which he approved. He found a law in his members warring against the law of his conscience, and bringing him into subjection to the law of sin which was in his members, and it was out of that condition he had obtained deliverance through Jesus Christ. The Apostle is here repeating what he had said in the first chapter. He had there boasted of the gospel of Christ, as a power by which men might rise out of unrighteousness, and he here boasts that the law of the spirit of life in Christ Jesus had made him free from the law of sin and death,—had given the victory to the law of his mind over the law in his members; and in the 3d verse he tells us that the law of the spirit of life in Christ Jesus has this power, through God's having sent His own Son in the likeness of sinful flesh, and having thus condemned sin in the flesh, that so the righteousness of the law might be fulfilled in us by our walking not after the flesh but after the spirit.

The Apostle, as we have seen, is not always careful to distinguish the objective from the subjective, the gospel *concerning* Christ from the faith and filial trust which the gospel is intended to produce; and this expression "the law of the spirit of life in Christ Jesus" might stand for either. Probably it here means filial trust, or spiritual-mindedness, inasmuch as the objective gospel follows immediately in the statement that God had sent His own Son in the likeness of sinful flesh. The law of the spirit of life in Christ will thus be Christ's own life, his own filial trust in the Father, communicated to us through the knowledge that His Father is our Father also, and that He so loved us as to give His only begotten Son to taste death for every man. "For what the law"—that law of the mind which he had spoken of in the preceding chapter—"could not do in that it was weak through the flesh,"—in that its operation was hindered by carnal insensibility to the great truth that the Lawgiver is our Father—God hath done, by sending His own Son in the likeness of sinful flesh and *for* sin, thus condemning sin in the flesh, that the righteousness of the law might be fulfilled in us by our walking not after the flesh but after the spirit.

What was the sin in the flesh which God condemned by sending His own Son in the likeness of sinful flesh? Want of filial trust is the radical sin of the flesh. God is a Spirit, and the flesh cannot discern Him. It is only the spiritual faculty that can discern the obligatory character of the law, but even this may be done without discerning God's fatherly purpose in giving the law, and therefore without acquiring power to obey it. This disbelief in love is the sin which God condemned by sending His Son in the likeness of sinful flesh. This act of unmistakeable love condemned the sin, by showing the unreasonableness of it—by showing that it was a lie. The sin consisted in disbelief of God's love, and He condemned it by this manifestation of love.

This thought must have been in the Apostle's mind when he wrote the passage, but another phase of the same thought would naturally occur to him also. Jesus was himself the pattern Truster; he trusted the Father in the extremity of suffering and death, and the Father, by setting him forth as our example, condemned the distrust of man, even as Noah is said to have condemned the unbelieving world by his own faith in God's warning of the coming flood.[1]

The object of God in condemning this distrust was "that the righteousness of the law might be fulfilled in us, by our walking not after the flesh but after the spirit." The flesh expects happiness from self-gratification, the spirit seeks its good in God and in conformity to His will. This is the righteousness of the law, which is fulfilled in us when we apprehend and accept the relations in which we stand to the spiritual world—it is fulfilled in the recognition of God as our Father, and of men as our brethren. The flesh, in seeking self-gratification and in its occupation with outward things, ignores these relations, and thus makes the law powerless even whilst its claim is acknowledged, and the law of the spirit of life in Christ Jesus gives the law its proper power by quickening in us the apprehension of these relations.

The antagonism between faith and works with which the epistle commences seems in this chapter to be merged in an antagonism

[1] Heb. xi. 7.

between the spirit and the flesh; the power which was before attributed to faith being here attributed to the spirit, and all that opposes faith, which before had been spoken of under the name of works, or the law, being here called the flesh.

The expression in chapter v., " when we were without strength," seems to correspond with the idea expressed in the 8th chapter, " What the law *could not do in that it was weak* through the flesh," for though in the one the weakness is ascribed to man, and in the other to the law, yet evidently it is the same weakness, as in both cases it is remedied by the knowledge of the love of God manifested in sending His Son to man's aid.

Throughout the chapter, as indeed through the whole of the New Testament, it is always assumed as a fact that flesh and spirit are co-existing elements in man's being, that in following the first he is the child of the devil and the servant of sin, and that in following the second he is the child of God and the servant of righteousness. Do we cease then to be the children of God when we follow the flesh? Certainly not. In becoming the children of the devil we sin, not only because his service is sin, but also because in choosing his service we are repudiating our true Father. The appearing of the Son of God in our flesh was the manifestation of his brotherhood towards us as a race, and thus it was a revelation that his Father is our Father. The prodigal did not cease to be his father's son when he went into the far country, and nothing but the thought that he had still a father in the old home-land could have brought him back. Assuredly while we are living in the selfish nature we are doing what we can to separate ourselves from the Father and the Son; but it was to reveal to us that in so living we are sinning against our true normal status, that is, against the relation to God, in which and for which we were created,—it was to condemn this sin in the flesh, and to bring us out of it,— that the Father sent the Son into the world to taste death for every man. "Though the hand say I am not of the body, is it therefore not of the body?"

The presence of the conscience in every man, however condemning it may be and however disregarded, is a satisfying demonstration of our organic relation to the Son of God, "the true Light which lighteth every man that cometh into the world," and our neglect of its admonitions does not destroy that relation. "Have they stumbled that they should fall? God forbid." The Apostle assumes that this is the condition of all men. He assumes that Christ is in them as the hope of glory, as the capacity of rising out of the flesh and living in the spirit, as the assurance that this is God's purpose concerning them which shall yet be fulfilled in every individual. And as he also assumes that they are carnal, and have a fleshly nature which needs to be striven against and brought under subjection to the spirit, he does not regard any present carnality as dissolving their relation to Christ, or as cutting off the hope of final glory, though in the meantime it does separate them from his fellowship, and must continue to do so as long as it remains unsubdued.

*   *   *   *   *

In the 14th verse we read, "As many as are led by the Spirit of God, they are the sons of God." The Spirit of the Son is led by the Spirit of the Father—"for ye have not received the spirit of bondage again to fear, but ye have received the spirit of sonship, whereby we cry, Abba, Father"—that spirit which by its very nature continually breathes out the first four clauses of the Lord's Prayer.

※   ※   ※   ※   ※

Chapter IX.

In this chapter the Apostle returns to a subject which he had before touched on, but had not fully searched to its results, I mean the apparent rejection of the Jewish people. This subject was not only specially interesting to him as a Jew, but was also connected with that trustworthiness in the character of God which he had held forth as the ground of faith or trust to all mankind, to Gentiles as well as Jews.

If the Jews were definitely cast away on account of their repudiation of the gospel, what confidence could a Gentile be warranted in placing in God's fatherly purpose towards him? If man's sin could exhaust the mercy of God there was every reason to fear that a very small residue would ultimately be saved. But then Habakkuk's prophecy of the earth being filled with the knowledge of the glory of God would lose the very pith of its meaning, and our Apostle's words in the concluding verses of the 5th chapter would be but empty sounds. He had been calling men to trust in an immoveable purpose of God towards the race, and that purpose is found not to be a universal purpose, but one liable to immense deductions! If this be so he feels that the whole gospel which he has been setting forth as the stable ground of the faith of all men, is in fact crumbling under their feet. To enable it really to bear the weight of the human race, its universality and its infallibility must be established.

If we enter in any measure into the fervid outburst of the Apostle at the conclusion of the 8th chapter we shall understand how, after giving vent to it, he is instantaneously led to contrast these high anticipations with the actual condition of the Jewish people. Were *they* not the special objects of God's foreknowledge and predestination? Had they not been selected from amongst the nations as witnesses for God? How then had they been permitted to fall into the enormity of rejecting His Son, who had come to bless them and all men by turning them from their iniquities, and so to accomplish the whole purpose of God for them and for the race?

There were many assuredly among the Roman disciples who, as they owed their first hope towards God to the Hebrew Scriptures, cherished warm feelings of reverence and gratitude to the nation from whom they had received those Scriptures. Whilst drinking in the Apostle's glowing words they might think he had forgotten his connection with the seed of Abraham for whom God had done such great things in times past, and that he was satisfying himself and trying to satisfy them, with a hope of glory from which that seed was excluded. St. Paul proceeds to answer these thoughts. He begins with strong asseverations of devoted love to his brethren according to the flesh, and of deep interest in their present condition; he emphatically dwells on their national distinctions and on the high place which God had given them in His dealings with the human race. He says not only that he has continual sorrow in his heart on account of them, but that he could wish to make himself an anathema for them, following the example of Christ, who had made himself an anathema for them and for all men.[1] He then goes on through the three wonderful chapters that follow, ix. x. xi., to explain the dealings of God with both Jews and Gentiles, and the purpose which He will most surely accomplish in them all by these dealings.

These chapters have been stumbling-blocks in the way of readers probably ever since they were written, and yet they are just the exposition of "the mercies of God," as the Apostle testifies, when at their conclusion he says in the beginning of the 12th chapter, " I beseech you therefore, brethren, by *the mercies of God,*" —by those very dealings of God, namely, which he has been unfolding to them—" that ye present your bodies a living sacrifice, holy and acceptable to God, which is your reasonable service." Let me here observe, in passing, that

---

[1] We fail to understand this passage when we read it in our mistranslated version, where it is thus rendered :—" I could wish that myself were accursed from Christ." It should rather be "following the leading of Christ," which is undoubtedly the meaning of the same preposition (ἀπό) in 2 Timothy i. 3 : "God whom I serve *from* my forefathers," that is, walking in their steps. Thus Paul desires to follow Christ in making himself a curse or anathema for his brethren,—not dreaming of separation from Christ, but desiring to partake in his curse, thereby entering into a closer union with him by a participation in his spirit of self-sacrificing love.

the first great principle which St. Paul pressed on us in the 8th chapter, and which is to be always borne in mind in meditating on the mercies of God, is that—although He is essentially and eternally a Father, a God of mercy and goodness and blessing,—His goodness *cannot* bless us until we yield up our hearts to Him, that is, until we are spiritually-minded. This transformation of heart is accordingly the great object of all His dealings with us, an object which He will never cease to urge by all means, in this and in every stage of our being, until it is accomplished; in accordance with that emphatic word in the parable, " He goeth after that which is lost *until he finds it.*"

The Apostle has not lost sight of the prophecy of Habakkuk, which is indeed the text of the whole epistle. We have seen how in that prophecy the assurance that all afflictions and calamities are intended " not for destruction but correction," so that finally " the earth shall be filled with the knowledge of the glory of God," is represented as the basis of the faith and consequently of the righteousness of man. He had begun his epistle by setting down this assurance as his starting-point, and in the 8th chapter we have seen how he returns to it, when he tells us that "the creature was made subject to vanity" for the one purpose of forcing it to take refuge in this hope, that "the creature shall be delivered from the bondage of corruption into the glorious liberty of the children of God," which is unquestionably the very assurance proclaimed by Habakkuk in his day. The eye of St. Paul, enlightened by faith, saw this blessed consummation across all the present darkness, and he could rejoice in it even as the old prophet did; he could calmly survey the darkness, and discern how it could not only be reconciled with the future glory, but be made by the overruling wisdom of God subservient to it.

It is this assurance of a gracious purpose of God in all things that can alone sustain us, as it did of old the prophet and the apostle, when we contemplate His dealings with our race or with the individuals who compose it. He is educating us by ways that we know not, but we know the end to which He is leading each one of us. He uses one man to subserve, in the education of others, as a beacon or an example, as a scourge or as a consolation; yet though He uses the man for these ends He does not then throw him away as if his own individual interests were unimportant. We have seen that trustful recipiency is the right condition for the creature, and to this condition God will bring us all through the consciousness of entire helplessness and even of sin, that so that blessed word (ch. xi. 32) may have its fulfilment, "For God hath concluded them all in unbelief, *that He might have mercy upon all;*" that is, that all may receive salvation, not as the fruit of their own deservings, but as the gift of God's free mercy.

"Is there then unrighteousness with God? God forbid!" (ix. 14.) This purpose of final blessing is the vindication of His righteousness in all His dealings with His creatures; this is what the Apostle means to teach in his quotation from Exodus, and in his commentary on it in the following verse. If we consider it well we shall see that it is a counterpart of Habakkuk's prophecy. I have said that Paul when he made that short quotation from Habakkuk, "The just shall live by faith," virtually referred to the whole prophecy; so also I believe that he here refers to the whole context—to chapters xxxii. xxxiii. xxxiv. of Exodus. We find there the record of Israel's sin in worshipping the calf, and of its punishment, and then we have the proclamation of the name of the Lord, " The Lord God, merciful and gracious, long-suffering, and abundant in goodness and truth, keeping mercy for thousands, forgiving iniquity and transgression and sin, and that will by no means clear the guilty; visiting the iniquity of the fathers upon the children unto the third and fourth generation, and" (filling up the quotation from the second commandment) " showing mercy unto thousands of them that love Him, and keep His commandments." This "name of God" is the same in substance with that which Habakkuk proclaimed when, in the prospect of the Chaldean invasion, he said, " O God, my holy One, we shall not die, Thou hast established them for correction." Moses saw that the essential character of God in relation to man is a mercy which does not "clear the guilty," —which does not cease to punish the sinner until he turns from his sin, until he has received correction. Such punishments are the visitations "unto the third and fourth generation," the needful temporary chastisements which lead to the mercies that are to rest for ever—on *the thousands of generations*—who through these chastisements have learned to love God and keep His commandments. Evidently as the limited period of the third and fourth generation is contrasted with the unlimited expanse of the thousand generations, so the passing inflictions are contrasted with the "everlasting mercies" which in due time shall cover the earth as the waters cover the sea.[1] The quotations from Hosea, as the attentive reader will perceive, guide our thoughts in the same direction.

It seems to me that this idea of a spiritual education for all men, continued through all stages of their being until the righteousness of God is fulfilled in them, is the real meaning of all Scripture, and the light which can alone guide us through these otherwise obscure chapters, and through all the obscure chapters of God's living dealings with ourselves and our fellow-men. Let us only keep hold of this great principle as expressed in the 32d

[1] See Isaiah liv. 7, 8.

verse of chapter xi., and we shall find all the graver difficulties disappear.

But let us go back for a moment to the 6th verse of chapter ix. and consider its connection with the preceding verses. The Apostle had been dwelling with true Jewish feeling on the high privileges of his nation. "To whom pertaineth the adoption, and the glory, and the covenants, and the giving of the law, and the service of God, and the promises; whose are the fathers, and of whom as concerning the flesh Christ came." And now he proceeds to show that all this is reconcilable with their present state. The vision undoubtedly seemed to tarry, but it had always done so, and they must wait for it. Through the whole course of their past history there had always been a marked division amongst them; there had been those who from the heart received the divine blessings, and there had been those whose hearts were wholly uninterested in them,—there had been a spiritual Israel and a carnal Israel. This distinction was typically set forth at the beginning by the election of Isaac and the rejection of Ishmael, and in like manner, in the next generation, by the election of Jacob and the rejection of Esau. And as it was only in the spiritual Israel that the purpose of God was really fulfilled, it might be supposed that the spiritual Israel alone constituted the true Israel, and that thus the promises of God to His people were really fulfilled when they were fulfilled to them. And yet the purpose of God embraced *the whole race, and could not attain its true absolute fulfilment* until the carnal become spiritual. "Blindness in part has" from the beginning "happened to Israel," but only "until the fulness of the Gentiles be come in, and so *all* Israel shall be saved, as it is written, There shall come out of Sion the Deliverer, and shall turn away ungodliness from Jacob," that is, He shall make the carnal Israel spiritual, and that in a way consistent with man's freedom, "Not by might nor by power, but by my Spirit, saith the Lord."

"Hath God cast away His people?" the Apostle asks, and the answer is "God forbid!" Yet in the following verse this emphatic negative seems to be somewhat modified—"God hath not cast away His people *which He foreknew*," which modification is explained and commented on down to the 7th verse, in which it is stated that "Israel hath not attained that which he seeketh for, but the election hath obtained it and the rest were blinded." Here then we have the elect portion of the Jewish people blessedly disposed of, and now the Apostle proceeds to consider the condition of those who did not belong to the election, whom he calls "*the rest who were blinded,*" and in speaking of whom he uses the sternest language which the Old Testament can supply; he speaks of them as those to whom "God had given the spirit of slumber, eyes that they should not see, and ears that they should not hear unto this day;" and of whom the prophet-king had said, "let their table be made a snare and a trap and stumbling-block unto them, let their eyes be darkened that they may not see, and bow down their back alway." Well, what is to become of these lost ones? What is to be their future? Why, the Apostle commences his exposition of their fate in this manner, "I say then, have they stumbled that they should fall? God forbid! but rather through their fall salvation is come unto the

Gentiles for to provoke them (the slumbering ones) to jealousy."

Now let me beg the reader to go over the whole passage again and satisfy himself that the persons against whom those stern denunciations are recorded are the same persons who are referred to in this confident tone. There can be no doubt that they are the same. And it is of them also that it is said, "If the casting away of them be the riches of the world, and the diminishing of them the riches of the Gentiles, how much more their fulness?" And again, "For if the casting away of them be the reconciling of the world, what shall the receiving of them be, but life from the dead?" This then, according to St. Paul, is the future history of the reprobates—the rejected, the lost—and he winds up his argument with that emphatic word, "For God hath concluded them all in unbelief, that He might have mercy upon all;" that is, as I have already said, that they might all feel that their salvation was the fruit of divine grace, not of human merit. After arriving at this conclusion he looks back on the way by which it has been attained with admiring wonder; he does not wonder at the mercy of God, but he wonders at the riches of the wisdom and knowledge which have brought about such a result by such means, making darkness light and crooked things straight.

There are three stages in the Epistle at which the triumphant feeling of the writer seems to reach the culminating-point—at which his far-seeing hope seems to overlook all intervening darkness, and to revel in the contemplation of a final result of universal blessedness. These stages occur in chapter v., in the latter part of chapter viii., and at the conclusion of chapter xi. In chapter v. from verse 18 to the end, and in chapter xi. from verse 32, we have light without a cloud or shadow, we have what appears to be an unequivocal revelation of an ultimate glory in which all are to participate. In chapter viii. an apparent limit is set to this hope, so that we are surprised to find the Apostle able to maintain the triumphant tone which distinguishes the concluding verses of the chapter. "We know," he says, "that all things work together for good *to them who love God, to them who are the called* according to His purpose; for whom He did *foreknow* He also did predestinate to be conformed to the image of His Son, that he might be the first-born among many brethren. Moreover, *whom He did predestinate* them He also called, and whom He called them He also justified, and whom He justified them He also glorified."

This language, according to a very common theology, and a verbal criticism which does not appear illogical, has been so interpreted as to imply that some are *not* foreknown and consequently can have no part in the glorious things spoken of in the following verses; and those who read it under the inspiration of this theology, instead of joining in the Apostle's triumph, are naturally led to ask the question, Are we among the foreknown? But is it not manifest that the Apostle expects the whole church to enter into his glorious anticipations? In the 21st verse he had said, "The *creature*"—that is, the whole creation, "shall be delivered from the bondage of corruption into the glorious liberty of the children of God," and here he goes back in thought to that deliverance, and invites all to rejoice in it, as the foreknowledge and purpose of God concerning all. This is the "hope" by which they were to be saved (see verse 24), and by which they were to be enabled to wait patiently for the accomplishment of the vision of which Habakkuk had said, "Though it tarry, wait for it, for at the end it will come, it will not tarry."

If we may judge by the tenor of the verses which follow (and this is surely our true guidance), the Apostle in writing the 29th verse could not have meant to awaken self-questionings, but rather to sweep away every fear and misgiving. It is evidently correlative to the 32d verse; the "foreknown" in the former are just the "all" in the latter, for whom God spared not His own Son. The tone of warning with which he concludes the 7th chapter and which he maintains through the first part of the 8th, is not intended to *limit* the hope, but to show *how* it is to be fulfilled. It is only through spiritual-mindedness, that is, through conformity to the image of the Son, that the ultimate glory is in any case to be reached; but God has predestined this preliminary condition also, and He will not slack His dealings with men until it is attained by all, as we find it distinctly declared in the four last verses of the 5th chapter that it shall be.

It seems to me that this view of the Apostle's

meaning in this passage is confirmed by the whole tenor of his thought in the three following chapters, in which, after having given utterance to his anticipations of the future glory and blessedness of the Christian church, he turns his eyes on his own countrymen. If there could be any class who should be excepted from the general statement made in the 32d verse, "He that spared not his own Son, but gave him up to the death for us all, how shall He not with him also freely give us all things?" it might be expected to be the Jewish race, who had crucified the Lord, and who ceased not to persecute all who put their trust in him, but there is no exception. God will use their very unbelief as the means whereby He will shut them up to the acknowledgment of their transgression, that so He may have mercy upon all. "O the depth of the riches both of the wisdom and knowledge of God! How unsearchable are His judgments, and His ways past finding out! For who hath known the mind of the Lord, or who hath been His counsellor? . . . . For of Him, and to Him, and through Him are all things, to whom be glory for ever. Amen."

FRAGMENTS.

I.—THE CLAIMS OF JESUS.
(Appendix A. Pages 9 and 40.)

In truth all the most striking declarations of the love of God which we meet with in the New Testament are based upon the supernatural claims of Jesus, and become vapid and unmeaning when these claims are set aside or ignored. Thus if Jesus was not the Son of God, in a sense peculiar to himself, how weak and pointless would such words as these be: "If God spared not His own Son, but gave him up to the death for us all, how shall He not with him also freely give us all things?" "God so loved the world that He gave His only begotten Son, that whosoever believeth on him might not perish, but have everlasting life;" or these: "God commendeth His love toward us, in that whilst we were yet sinners Christ died for us." The power and life of these and similar declarations lie entirely in the assumed fact that Jesus was one with the Father; the gift of the only begotten Son is set before us as the *measure* of the Father's love, and consequently if

Jesus was not the Son in a special sense, their whole meaning disappears. Unless he was a divine person, his love for men, manifested in every action of his life, could not be a direct revelation of the Father's love; it might even be considered greater than the Father's, self-sacrifice being the highest of all love. " Greater love hath no man than this, that a man lay down his life for his friends."

As a mere man, moreover, Christ could only have addressed the conscience, and set before it a duty to perform; he would not have been himself a foundation on which we might confidently rest—a fountain from which we might draw living strength enabling us to perform the duty. Whereas if he was really one with the Father, he is at once the revelation of God's paternal relation to us, and of *His* self-sacrificing love. In fact I believe that the vital dynamic efficiency of Christianity lies wholly in the discovery which it makes of the divine Sonship of Jesus Christ. Any wise human teacher might have taught his fellow-men that God was their Father, and they all brethren. Doubtless these are good and true words, but something more than words was needed; and to supply that need, when God would teach men His own universal Fatherhood and their relation of sonship to Him, and of brotherhood to one another, He sent forth the eternal Son, the Fountain of sonship, that by his assumption of their nature under all its sinless conditions of weakness and suffering and death, he might claim them as his brethren and as his Father's children. He claims them as having been created in him; he claims them as their Head, as the vine claims the branches, assuring them that they possess in him both a status of sonship and a communion of the spirit of sonship.

He thus opens up to us the spiritual world, revealing that self-sacrificing love is the law which binds its elements together. The Father sacrifices self in giving up the Son—the Son in giving himself—and from him the whole spiritual creation, constituted in him, as its organic Head, is supplied with that same spirit of self-sacrificing love, which can alone maintain order and harmony throughout.

II.—"BLESSED ARE THE POOR IN SPIRIT."

(Appendix B. Page 20.)

I AM sure there must be many who have a difficulty in understanding these words of our Lord. It must almost seem to them as if he had meant to pronounce a blessing on the cowardly and mean-spirited; whereas the blessing is on those who know and keep their place in the divine hierarchy.

We are dependent creatures, not self-existent or self-sufficing; but there is nothing degrading in this dependence, for we share it with the eternal Son.

When we forget this, we lose our blessedness, for it consists in the spirit of sonship, by which alone we can receive and respond to our Father's love. God does not call for the acknowledgment of our dependence as a mere homage to His sovereignty, but because we are His children, and it is only through this acknowledgment that we can receive His fatherly love and blessing. The blessedness arises out of the spirit of dependence, and when that spirit departs the blessedness departs with it; therefore as the spirit of independence is the spirit of this world,[1] we need not wonder at its unblessedness, for that spirit shuts the heart against God, and cuts off its supply from the Fountain of life.

III.—WHAT IS RIGHTEOUSNESS?
(Appendix C. Page 106.)

THIS is a question more easily asked than answered. Is righteousness something absolute, or is it relative? Assuredly it is difficult to conceive of a righteousness without relations; perhaps it is impossible. When we think of the righteousness of God, we think of it as eternal and unchangeable, yet not as

---

[1] When I say that the spirit of independence is the spirit of this world, I do not mean that men would distinctly assert their independence of God, and avowedly cast off their dependence on Him, but that *in fact* they do not depend on Him, *i.e.* they look to *other* sources for their supply and enjoyment.

altogether independent of relations, for we can scarcely think of it except as characterising His purpose in creation and His treatment of His creatures, which implies the idea of relation. God sees each human being different from every other, and His thought and acting towards them are *righteous*, because He has respect to this difference. Farther, I believe that nothing so fills up our conception of God's righteousness as the idea of pure unselfish love, and love by the necessity of its nature is relative.

Righteousness in man is evidently relative, yet not on that account either arbitrary or conventional. Certain outward acts, which are by common consent recognised as the indications of inward right feelings or purposes, may and doubtless do vary in different places and circumstances, but still we know that truth and honesty and unselfish kindness and manliness are the substantial elements of moral worth, and that these must be the same at all times and in all places.

Righteousness is not constituted such by authority, but by everlasting truth. In one of Plato's dialogues, the question is raised, "Whether is an act holy because it pleases the gods, or does it please the gods because it is holy?" and although no final solution is arrived at, yet it is manifest that the author intends his readers to choose the second alternative.

I believe that to the Jewish mind the connection

between morality and an acknowledgment of the will of God appeared more necessary and vital than it does to the European mind; and in accordance with this, I am inclined to think that St. Paul would have treated that question about holiness as a mere play upon words. Yet he would have strongly felt that it was not God's power but His holiness which authorises and stamps and supplies holiness in the creature.

But when I say that the Jewish mind had a stronger sense of the connection between all morality and a recognition of the will of God than is felt amongst ourselves, do I mean to say that this was merely a national idiosyncrasy, arising out of special circumstances in the national physiology and history, and that the European view of the matter is the truer? Very far from it; I believe, on the contrary, that true morality can never be separated from a knowledge and a recognition of the place which we hold in the spiritual cosmos, and that there can be no true theory of moral sentiments, no true moral philosophy, which is not based on this knowledge; and I may add that the exceeding barrenness of European literature in this particular province, seems to me a most decisive proof that our thinkers have not taken the right path when they have attempted to expound ethics apart from theology.

IV.—JUSTIFICATION.

So long as we think of men as a mere mass of individuals, we shall find it difficult to form a definite idea of righteousness or justification. But when we think of them as members of a family of which God is the Father, the difficulty is removed; righteousness is then seen to be healthful order; filial trust in relation to the Father extending itself in brotherly love to the rest of the family. If this be the true view of man's condition, manifestly there can be no other righteousness, no other real morality, but this order. Manifestly also this order in not righteousness in consequence of its being judged or imputed as righteousness by God, but is so essentially, making itself felt by the man who possesses it to be his right state, just as a dislocated joint at once feels its *justification* or rectification when it is restored to its proper position. That is to say, the man does not need to reason thus: "God calls me to filial trust, and approves of it as my right state, and therefore, as I am exercising this trust, I may *infer* that I am in my right state, that is, justified." He does not need to reason thus, for his filial trust proves its own rightness by reducing the dislocation and giving him ease, thus consciously putting him in his right state. I believe that this is the meaning of the word *justified* in the parable of the Pharisee and the Publican (Luke xviii. 14). The self-flattery of the Pharisee could not really give him ease, because it did not reduce the dislocation,—it did not put him in his right place in relation to God; whilst the Publican's confession of unworthiness, and his casting of himself simply on the mercy of God, at once put him in his right position—a position which proves its rightness by its perfect peace—he went to his house *justified* rather than the other.

This is the justification that we need—the reduction of all our dislocations—the rightening in us of all that is wrong, delivering us from self-seeking, and filling us with love. If we see that filial trust in God is the only principle which can accomplish this great thing, we shall at once recognise that it has as much the stamp of God upon it as the law of gravitation in the material world has.

V.—FORGIVENESS.

When St. Paul spoke of justification by faith, he meant to say that filial trust in God as a loving and righteous Father is the real essential righteousness of man—that it will make him a good man, a good neighbour, a good citizen; and he also meant to say that no man could have this trust except through the conviction that God is unchangeably his Father.

There is no room here for imputation, in the sense usually given to that word. Its sense in the Bible itself is simply that in the judgment of God such filial trust *is* righteousness.

This is no question of words, for if the righteousness of faith be a mere conventionality, though God Himself were the author of that conventionality, it cannot be the ultimate good intended for man; it cannot permanently satisfy his spirit. It is moreover evidently absurd to suppose that this faith is followed or *rewarded* by forgiveness, for it cannot exist without the assurance of forgiveness, that is, without the assurance of an infinite and unchanging love, which even in punishing seeks our good.

It is difficult for a man conscious of deep sin to maintain this assurance—to believe that notwithstanding all his transgressions, God is still his loving, forgiving Father,—and yet till he believes this he can never pray a son's prayer, nor have a son's feeling towards God. We must have this assurance as our starting-point in the path of righteousness, we must *begin* by having it, we cannot make a single step without it, because filial trust is our righteousness, and filial trust is impossible without an absolute and unwavering assurance of forgiveness. Forgiveness, therefore, must be a permanent fact in the relation of God to man; not a thing which our faith creates, but a thing which exists whether we believe it or not, a condition of things in which we live, and which our faith—or I would rather here say our spiritual reason—perceives and lays hold of as an existing reality, and as such rests on.

The intelligent belief that we are under a process of education in filial righteousness—the belief that this was God's purpose in creating us, and that our sins have not induced Him to abandon it—would, if really held, necessarily involve the assurance that forgiveness is man's permanent condition, because such a purpose could not be carried on without a continual forgiveness; and it would at the same time help us to understand that it is however a forgiveness which by no means excludes punishment, though it uses all punishment for the correction and essential good of the transgressor. But we find by experience that our fears are too strong for our logic. The sense of sin creates distrust, and therefore God, to overcome this distrust, has in the gospel shown us the eternal foundation of all trust, by opening up to us the mystery of His own nature of Father and Son, and by revealing to us that we are created in the Son, who is thus the root and type and mould of our being, and also the assured pledge of the Father's relation to us, and of His purpose for us. He has given him to die for us, that in that act we might have the measure of His love.

VI.—THE GOSPEL NO CHANGE IN THE PURPOSE OF GOD.

ARE we to think that when Paul proclaimed the gospel, he meant to teach that God had now changed His tone and adopted a more loving method of dealing with His moral creatures than in the former times? Assuredly he can have had no such meaning; he must mean to say that the gospel gives the true representation of the unchangeable character of God, and that it was the ignorance of men that made them think otherwise of Him. There was a progress in the teaching—no change in the character or purpose of the Teacher.

The light in man's conscience which condemns his sin ought to be understood by him to be "the goodness of God leading him to repentance." But man misinterprets that condemning light, and calls it not the goodness but the enmity of God. And therefore God in His mercy has met this misinterpretation by sending that light of the conscience (in the person of His Son) into the world, in the likeness of sinful flesh, to seek and to save the lost, thus giving the fullest manifestation of His fatherly purpose. For the discovery that there exists a filial nature in God, and that conscience testifies of the indwelling presence in man of that filial nature, is the peculiar doctrine of Christianity, a doctrine communicated to us, not that we may be rewarded for believing it, but that through the belief of it we may know the place which we hold in the heart and purpose of God, and be brought into perfect sympathy with that heart and purpose.

VII.—GOD'S PURPOSE FOR US IS RIGHTEOUSNESS.

God sees us as we are, yet with a love that always desires to make us—what we should be—like Himself; and which will eternally persist in urging the accomplishment of that desire. It is this characteristic of God's love which alone makes it worthy of trust. A love which does not seek return is not really love, and a righteousness which does not seek to make others righteous is not really righteousness.

If we saw a father punishing his child, and when we asked him what effect he expected to produce he were to answer, I don't think of that, I only think of what he has deserved, should we not at once say that he was neither a loving father nor a righteous man?

So long as I believe that God's condemnation of my sin is not connected with this purpose, and that He punishes me merely *because I deserve it*, it is impossible to trust Him; but when I understand that His condemnation contains within it an unchangeable purpose to draw me out of my sin, I can accept

His condemnation and bless Him for it. It seems to me that the Gospel of Jesus Christ is just the full and living manifestation of this purpose,—that it means this or nothing.

VIII.—THE MEANING OF SALVATION.

WE should ask what is the meaning of the word *salvation*. For most assuredly the spirit and character of our religion will much depend on the signification which we attribute to it. If we really believe that the great object of the Saviour's mission to this earth was to save men from their sins, we shall also believe that salvation means a deliverance not from punishment but from sin. And how is this to be effected? How can we escape from sin? I would answer that the only conceivable way is by ceasing from sin, that is, by becoming righteous. And as we have seen that man's righteousness consists in filial trust, we seem to be conducted to the idea, that Christ saves us from sin, by revealing to us the trustworthiness of the Father.

IX.—THE FATHER REVEALED IN THE SON.

IF there be really in the Divine nature an only begotten Son, one with the Father, who is also the beginning or Head of the spiritual creation, the necessary inference is, that the relations of fatherhood and sonship are the fundamental principles which regulate and harmonise that creation. The revelation of the Son is the only thorough revelation of the Father; and as the Son is the Head of the spiritual creation, he of necessity communicates his own relation of Sonship to all its members; and as a common sonship is a common brotherhood, he also unites them all to each other in that bond. Thus love is the universal living law, originating with the Father and received by the Son, that it may by him be propagated to the whole spiritual family.

The revelation of the Son is the revelation of the universal sonship, a sonship which has not been forfeited by sin; for the appearance of Jesus on the earth and his assumption of our nature, under all its conditions of temptation and suffering and mortality, gives the fullest and most absolute demonstration that our sin had not made God cease to be our Father, or abandon His purpose of training us into a participation of the Son's character and blessedness. And this demonstration was necessary, for a sense of unforgiven sin is incompatible with the trust which constitutes filial goodness.

The appearance of Christ in our nature is in itself a declaration of the forgiveness of sin; not that forgiveness is *attainable*, but that it exists as a permanent fact in the Divine nature, and a permanent element in the relation of God to man. It is a witness that His love survives our sin, and that His punishments are not for destruction but for correction. When we are sure of this, we can trust ourselves in His hands, accepting any punishment He may be pleased to send, assured that fatherly love is the unwilling but wise inflictor of it, and therefore we can love Him even though we know that we have sinned against Him.

Man has lost his place in the spiritual order by ceasing to believe in the Father's love, and so feeling himself constrained to seek his good in self-gratification; and as he had thus lost it, he could only recover it by having that love forced (as it were) upon him in such a form as to draw him out of his self-seeking. And such, indeed, is the form of that love of God which is revealed in Jesus Christ. The principle of self-sacrifice underlies all true love. It may remain undiscerned, and until discerned the love may seem questionable; but when it really is recognised, the worst of men are affected by it. "All these have of their abundance cast into the treasury, but she of her penury hath cast in all that she had, even all her living." This is the human type, and the Divine original is "God so loved the world that He gave His only begotten Son," that whosoever believeth in Him—whosoever, that is, believeth in this self-sacrificing love—might not perish, but have, in that very belief, eternal life. "He that spared not His own Son, how shall He not with him freely give us all things? Scarcely for a righteous man will one die, but God commendeth His love towards us, in that, whilst we were yet sinners, Christ died for us." Such is the Father's love.

The connection between these three great principles, (1) the eternal Sonship, (2) faith or dependent recipiency, and (3) that sacrifice of self which is the only putting away of sin, is to me an irrefragable evidence of the truth of the whole revelation. I see that sin can be put away only by this self-sacrifice; that filial trust is the only principle which can produce such sacrifice; and that this trust must exist within the Divine nature itself. And thus these three great doctrines of Christianity, the Divine nature of Christ, the righteousness of faith, and the necessity of self-sacrifice, appear to be cognate principles existing as necessary elements of the spiritual order, and in perfect harmony with the reason and conscience of man.

This is the true *natural* religion, which carries God's own certificate to my reason.

X.—THE TRUST OF CHRIST.

CHRIST come in the flesh, lived a life of faith or trust in his Father. As the Head and Representative of men he trusted in the Father's purpose of deliverance for the race, and in this trust he yielded himself up to the power of that purpose, so that it was accomplished in him. And he did this that all men might apprehend the trustworthiness of the Father and the power of a real trust in Him, and might thus be strengthened and encouraged to partake in his trust, that so they might also partake in its results.

The righteousness of God towards man consists in this loving purpose, and the righteousness of man towards God consists in his faith in that purpose, a trust which makes man a fellow-worker with God in carrying it out. The eternal Son came into our world to reveal the Fatherhood of God; none but a Son could have made such a revelation, and none but those who are created in the Son's nature could be capable of comprehending or receiving it. He came to draw and guide the hearts of the children to their Father by revealing the fatherliness of the Father's heart, and he did this by his own unfaltering trust even whilst standing in their place, accepting and enduring that penalty which they had incurred.

XI.—CHRIST THE HEAD OR REPRESENTATIVE OF MAN (ἡ ἀρχή τῆς κτίσεως).

APART from outward revelation, is there anything in human experience to help us in the apprehension of this doctrine, of the truth of which St. Paul had probably an intuitive perception? It seems to me that the argument in the fifth chapter of Romans, from verse 12 to the end, gives the answer to this question, by referring to a fact in our nature which at once suggests the idea of the doctrine as its correlative.

It is certain that we inherit qualities both of mind and body from our progenitors—often bad qualities; above all, we inherit death. We also feel that from some quarter or other we inherit conscience—the apprehension of righteousness, and the sense of its obligatory character. But we cannot refer the evil and the good to the same source; we must then have two descents—two fountains of life; there must be two heads of the race. Those of my readers who adopt the Bible history of Adam, and believe that God permitted the poison of sin and its penalty to be transmitted from our carnal head to us his descendants, will at once feel that much more is it to be credited that in the Divine purpose there is a spiritual Head from whom spiritual health and blessing, resurrection and eternal life, may likewise be transmitted to all men. But even those who have doubts as to the headship of Adam in respect to all men, can scarcely doubt of the oneness of conscience in all men, and hence we are logically conducted to the idea of a personal fountain of righteousness as the Head of men.

I believe that this idea was in the Apostle's mind from the beginning of the epistle, and that when he represented the revelation of the Divine righteousness of faith as the chief boast of the gospel, he thought of it as commencing with the eternal Son, and laid up in him as its fountain, from whom it was ever flowing out, and seeking entrance into all men; and therefore that it was in realising their union with him, and their relation through him to the Father, that they could best learn the great lesson of faith.

Faith in the Son as the Head and Root of humanity, in whom men were created, thus becoming partakers of his nature—the Divine favour which rested ever on him resting also on them as the overshadowing firmament under which all are born, and under which all live—this faith appeared to Paul to be the explanation of and guide into faith in the Father. And this I believe is the meaning of that benediction with which he concludes all his epistles—" The grace of our Lord Jesus Christ "—not the grace which he *bestows*, but that which he *receives*, the grace in which he himself stands—" be with you all." This is his usual formula; and in 2 Cor. he simply expands it, specifying the elements of which it consists, namely, the love of God, and the communion of the Holy Spirit.

XII.—THE SACRIFICE WHICH PUTS AWAY SIN.

In the Epistle to the Hebrews, Christ is said to have put away sin by the sacrifice of himself. I believe that nothing but this sacrifice of self can in any case put sin away, and that Christ, as the Head of the race, made this sacrifice that it might be reproduced in every member of his body. It was trust in his Father's righteous love which produced it in him, and nothing but the same trust can produce it in any one. Therefore, whilst showing in his own life a continual example of that trust, he was at the same time continually declaring the trust-worthiness and love-worthiness of the Father.

A son may reveal a father in two ways; either by being like him—so entirely in his image as to be justified in saying, He that hath seen me hath seen my father—or by manifesting a constant reverential, loving trust, and thus testifying that the father is worthy of such trust. Jesus revealed the Father in both these ways. He could say, "If you can trust my love you may trust His, for in mine you see His;" and he could also say, "I know Him so well that I have an unfaltering trust that everything He appoints for me is with a purpose of infinite love. That trust makes everything easy. It has made my yoke easy and my burden light; and if you knew Him as I desire to reveal Him to you, it would do the same for you." This is the meaning of that beautiful word (Matt. xi. 28), " Come unto me, all ye that labour and are heavy laden, and I will give you rest." The 27th verse is the key to all which follows : " No man knoweth the Father save the Son, and he to whom the Son will reveal Him." Jesus is the revealer of the Father, and if men will believe in the revelation, they will become partakers of his rest; their yoke also will become easy and their burden light.

XIII.—LIFE THROUGH DEATH.

The promise to Abraham of a son in his old age was associated with the hope of the final triumph of good over evil in the world ; " in thy seed shall all the families of the earth be blessed ;" and thus his faith was not a mere confidence that the promise of a son would be fulfilled, but was faith in a righteous God, in a Being whose desire and purpose is righteousness. Afterwards, when called by God to offer up this promised son, he was strengthened to obey by falling back on the fact that God had already proved His power and trustworthiness by giving him that son, and hence concluding that He could restore him to life even from the dead. He gave to God a full faith, and in heart a full obedience, though his hand was stayed from the execution. He seems to have been taught by this dealing of God, to look for the accomplishment of the promised blessing through death.

And this is the character of Christian faith; it is faith in God, who led His Son *through death* into new life;—through a death which, as due to sin, he by assuming our nature had incurred, into a life which he had taken hold of by filial trust, and which the righteous purpose of God bestows on us also through our participation in his trust.

The sentence of sorrow and death *is not to be set aside, but passed through*, and the foregone sins, though pretermitted and passed over,—that is, not regarded by God as reasons for abandoning His purpose of training us in righteousness,—must yet receive their penalty.

XIV.—THE DEATH OF CHRIST—JUDAS.

The death of Christ on the cross, as submitted to by him in fulfilment of his Father's will, was an act of self-sacrificing love, and was thus a manifestation of the true nature of righteousness. But it was more than this; it was apparently the death of a criminal—the execution of a penal sentence. He had assumed a nature which, through sin, had fallen under the condemnation of death, and being thus under condemnation, he voluntarily accepted death, thereby acknowledging its righteousness. He did this as the well-beloved Son and Revealer of the Father, and as the Head and Representative of men; thereby declaring that the Father, even when pronouncing and executing the sentence of death on man, had not abandoned His purpose of training him into righteousness, and that man in accepting death yields himself to that purpose.

The Father sent the Son to pass through man's suffering life and death to prove that whilst He saw it to be right and inevitable that sin should be visited by sorrow and death, His love ceased not to rest on those who were thus visited; and that it was therefore at once their right and their duty to trust in that love throughout the whole process.

Sin begins with distrust of God. The sinner believes that following his own will and not God's is the way of happiness, and having thus left his true position, the consciousness of sin increases his distrust; he feels that he has forfeited the right to trust God, that trusting now would seem like a denial that he had sinned. Thus even the right feeling which remains in him seems to forbid trust, and yet trust is his only possible righteousness!

The assurance, then, that God ever remains his loving Father is the gospel which in all circumstances man needs in order to his being righteous, and this is the gospel which is given him in Jesus

Christ—a gospel which assures him that it is right—even when lying under the consciousness and the punishment of sin—to trust in the love of God. It was the want of this trust which made Peter deny his Lord, and nothing but the reawakening of trust could bring him out of his sin. It would have been right for Judas to have had that trust the moment after he had betrayed his Lord. Such a trust, containing, as it must have done, such an untold amount of self-abhorrence, would, we believe, have been a higher and deeper trust than he had ever had before.

It is indeed difficult to conceive how Judas, even in the exercise of such a trust, could through eternity arrive at peace, with such a memory ever present with him. We can scarcely conceive how even the fullest forgiveness of God could enable him to forgive himself, or purge his memory of its mortal agony. It is evident that the purer we become we must increasingly abhor and loathe all sin, especially in ourselves; and thus it would appear that if memory remains in the future stages of our being, the retrospect of past transgression must become ever increasingly painful to us. Yet we cannot doubt but that there must be a sufficient antidote in the Divine love even for this form of agony,—a power to give perfect peace even to a Judas when he turns to God. I believe that it is our ignorance of the nature of Divine love—of its power and sweetness and blessedness—which makes it so difficult for us to conceive of such a deliverance. And as that love, though it passes the reason to conceive it, is yet in harmony with reason, we may suppose that one of its consolations to a Judas will be, not only that God has brought a blessing to the world out of his transgression, but that, through the very horror of that fearful act, his own soul has been brought into a deeper trust in God, and thus into a deeper righteousness than, it may be, he could otherwise have attained.

XV.—SIN.

I SHOULD feel myself sinning against God and my own conscience if I were either in thought or expression to palliate the evil of sin. The enormous misery in the world (evidently the consequence of sin) marks God's estimate of it; yet it seems to me that the fact of His choosing to encounter all this sin and all this misery with the view of educing from it righteousness in man, marks also that in His judgment it is worth while going through the process in order to arrive at the result. It cannot be from a necessity in the nature of things, but must be according to God's own purpose in constructing man, that evil tendencies are transmitted from parent to child, and are thus indefinitely multiplied.

Are we not from this fact compelled to conclude that the spiritual education of man is to be carried on through a conflict with such tendencies, and through the self-condemnations arising out of our failures in resisting temptations and our transgressions in abandoning ourselves to them? And thus the sense of sin requiring mercy, and the sense of weakness requiring help, seem to be the great means whereby we are trained to cast ourselves upon God. We must thus accept both the fact of the deep culpability of sin, and also the fact that it is used by God as an instrument of education.

These ideas must have been present to the mind of the Apostle when he put the question, Shall we continue in sin that grace may abound? and when he spoke of the abounding of sin leading to the superabounding of grace. It must always be wrong to do wrong, and wrong must always be worthy of condemnation; and yet it is possible that there is a righteousness educible from wrong—that is, from an experience of sin—of a higher order than could otherwise have been attained. It may seem as if this were making a difference between our righteousness and the righteousness of Christ, but I do not think that it is so, because the object of this process is to train man into that dependence on the Father which belongs to the very essence of the eternal Son. I do not attempt any further explanation of the difficulty.

XVI.—INNATE GOOD AND EVIL.

THE spiritual education of a man depends as much on the internal qualities with which he is born as on the external circumstances of his lot, and of course the success of the education must depend on his own apprehension and just appreciation of these internal qualities. There is a great mistake on this subject, into which we are exceedingly apt to fall, both in judging of ourselves and in judging of others. That of which we are most proud in ourselves, and which we most admire in others, is *spontaneity*—something which has been born with us—natural kindliness and generosity, unconscious self-sacrifice, and such like, preferring these to any qualities which have been produced by culture and effort; and that of which we are most ashamed in ourselves, and which we most condemn in others, is innate evil tendencies which appear to have been born with us. Yet certainly right reason would lead to an opposite judgment; and our true wisdom would be to consider the presence of that innate evil within us as permitted for the sake of our spiritual education, and consequently as a call from God to take hold of His strength, in order that we may successfully fight the good fight of faith against it. Learning by experience that dependence upon God is the true and only righteousness of the creature, we should thus advance in meetness for our appointed place in the body of His Son.

XVII.—THE TRUE IDEA OF "NATURAL RELIGION."

I REMEMBER well the satisfaction I felt on first reading the works of William Law. I felt as if I had found a great treasure, for I perceived that he regarded Christianity, not as a system of doctrines imposed on us by God, of which we could know nothing except from the Scriptures, but as the eternally true and natural religion to which all our spiritual faculties are adapted, and the intrinsic truth and certainty of which, though we could not have discovered it for ourselves, yet when revealed we can so apprehend, as to hold it on account of that intrinsic truth, and not on any outward authority whatsoever.

I at once came to accept this idea, and have ever since cherished it, as containing fundamental truth and most important guidance. I felt that when thus apprehended I really *believed* the doctrines of Christianity, and that until I did so apprehend them I could not be said really to believe them at all. I also felt that when God was pleased to reveal anything concerning Himself, it was impossible that He could be satisfied with our receiving it in the way of mere submissive obedience, and that He must mean us to understand and sympathise with His *purpose* in the revelation. Besides, I saw that the truest doctrines could be of no *use* to us until thus apprehended. If they were to affect the character, it was evidently only thus that they could do so; and what other purpose could they be intended to serve? Would it not be almost profane to suppose that we are called on to accept them merely as an exercise of submission? For what is a doctrine, and what is its use? Christian doctrine, as distinct from precept, means simply a discovery of the relation in which God stands to man, implying of course a revelation of His nature and character, so far as we are capable of apprehending them, inasmuch as our relation to Him necessarily depends on His nature and character. I cannot know my duties to any one, I cannot think of him, feel towards him, act towards him rightly, until I know the relation in which I stand to him. I believe that this is the true and only meaning of all religious dogmas. We are created in certain relations to God and to the spiritual world, and we have capacities and aptitudes suited to those relations, just as we have material organs suited to their objects; and the test of a true religion is that it gives such a representation of those relations as commends itself to our deepest consciousness. The doctrines of Christianity, if it is the true religion, must contain this representation. How then, in dealing with other minds, can we justify or defend the truth of the representation? In the last resort I believe our only real argument must consist in reproducing to them in our life the impression made by it on our own reason and conscience. "Ye are my witnesses, saith the Lord" (Isa. lxiii. 10).

XVIII.—"BY THIS SHALL ALL MEN KNOW THAT YE ARE MY DISCIPLES."

LET us for a moment contemplate the effect that thorough belief of their relationship to God would necessarily produce on the characters of men. They would feel that they were ever near to a loving Father who, though ordering the universe, and Himself the fountain out of which all things flow, yet thinks of each of them and cares for each with an unfailing love which is continually seeking fellowship with them, a love which can tolerate no sin, yet forgives all sin and strives to cast it out. They would feel that they possessed a treasure in this their Father's love above compare with any earthly good—a treasure which could never cease to satisfy them, and which could never be taken from them; yet they would not be lifted out of their human relations and duties by it, for they would feel that, as their Father orders all things in wisdom as well as in love, there must be a special fitness in the circumstances of their lot, whether pleasant or painful, to educate them for their high calling, and they would gather the instruction intended for them by a patient and dutiful watchfulness over each step of their way. They would love each other because they would see in every man a beloved child of their common Father.

And not only would the recognition of their high relationship produce such feelings, but according to the measure and activity of their faith—that recipient faculty by which the divine life is circulated through the body—they would receive the inflow of the spirit of the Son, disposing and enabling them to do all their Father's will.

I am sure that a *real* belief in our relationship to the Father through the Son would produce these results, and therefore, though I am most sensible of the difficulty of grasping it as a reality, and of the discouraging impression naturally and necessarily made by the faults of those who profess to believe it, I desire to hear this gospel proclaimed through the world, assured that it will prove itself to be *the power of God unto salvation* wherever it is really received.

It is a gospel which may be carried with equal suitableness to the bosoms and business of all classes of the community. It will help every man to do his work and bear his burden by showing him why the work and the burden were appointed. It will rescue him from the fluctuating uncertainties of time by giving him a secure standing-place in the eternal purpose of God. It will give him peace under the accusations of his own inner man by showing him that his Father can use even the agonies of conscious guilt to break down the barriers which self-reliance opposes to the reign of His Will.

www.ingramcontent.com/pod-product-compliance
Lightning Source LLC
Chambersburg PA
CBHW032002230426
43672CB00010B/2240